KNOW YOUR CALLING IN THE FIVEFOLD MINISTRY

Apostle Steve Lyston

Edited by: Marsha A. McCormack

Know Your Calling In The Fivefold Ministry

Copyright © 2020 by Apostle Steve Lyston.

Library of Congress Control Number: 2019954701
ISBN: 9781732076266

All Rights Reserved. No part of this publication may be reproduced, or transmitted in any form or by any means, electronic or mechanical including photocopying, recording or by any information storage and retrieval system, without prior permission in writing from the copyright owner.

Edited by: Marsha A. McCormack
Cover Design by: Johann D. A. Williams

Scripture quotations are taken from the New King James Version/Thomas Nelson Publishers, Nashville: Thomas Nelson Publishers. Copyright © 1982. Used by permission. All rights reserved.

This book was printed in Columbia, South Carolina in the United States of America

DEDICATION

This book is dedicated to all those men and women in Fivefold Ministry and those who earnestly seek to know more about the Fivefold Ministry and identify their calling.

This book is also dedicated to both Christians and non-Christians who want to know more about their calling.

THANK YOU

To the Holy Spirit for allowing the privilege of releasing this work, and for granting the inspiration, foresight and insight in this work.

To my family, Michelle, Shevado, Hannah, and Joshua – for every sacrifice you have made and all that had to be endured to allow God's work to be accomplished.

Bishop Dr. Doris Hutchinson for your continued and invaluable support in prayer and encouragement.

Pastor Nadra Brotherton for your prayerful support and encouragement.

Pastor Sophia DiMuccio for your continued prayers and invaluable support.

Pastor Omanso Jolly for your prayers and media support.

Pastor Maureen Phillips for allowing God to use you as He did Dorcas. Your support is invaluable.

Minister Letisha Livingstone for your invaluable assistance in the preparation of this book.

Deaconess Therese Forbes for your invaluable assistance in the preparation of this book.

Deaconess Marsha Hill for your consistent and invaluable support in all areas.

Apostle Jeffery Shuttleworth and the TBC Radio Family for your consistent support through prayer and media; and for stirring a greater urgency for the release of this book.

Mrs. Marsha McCormack for your faithful and consistent support.

Mr. Johann Williams for your loyalty and your consistent support.

The RWOMI Watchman Team for your consistent, prayerful support.

The RWOMI Humanitarian Outreach Team for your consistent support.

TABLE OF CONTENTS

Foreword

Introduction

Chapter 1	The Fivefold Ministry	12
Chapter 2	The Joel 2 Outpouring	17
Chapter 3	The Gifts Explained	22
Chapter 4	Understanding The In-Filling Of The Holy Spirit And Speaking In Tongues	37
Chapter 5	Who Is An Apostle	50
Chapter 6	Prophets And Protocol	67
Chapter 7	The Struggles Of A Prophet	87
Chapter 8	Wisdom And Protocol For Local Pastors	98
Chapter 9	Order In The Church: Sexual Purity	103
Chapter 10	False Grace Within The Fivefold	111
Chapter 11	Know The Scope Of Your Calling	119

Chapter 12 Called To Ministry	123
Chapter 13 The Watchman	130
Chapter 14 Apostasy And The Signs of Times	136
Chapter 15 Identifying Deception	140
Chapter 16 Death In The Pot! Beware Of False Doctrines	149
Chapter 17 Destroying The Counsel of Balaam	156
Chapter 18 Gospel Artists And Musicians Are Not Nightclub Entertainers	158
Chapter 19 Jezebel In The Fivefold	162
Chapter 20 God Still Speaks	170
Chapter 21 Follow God's Instructions	182
Chapter 22 Miracles And Instructions	186
Chapter 23 More On The Gifts	193
Chapter 24 Predestined For Purpose	201
Activity 1: Test Your Knowledge	209

Activity 2: Write The Prophetic
          Word   210

Activity 3: Record The Dreams   211

Bibliography   213

FOREWORD

Many people go through life not knowing what their true purpose really is; many have gone to the grave not fulfilling God's plans for their lives. Some have even felt the deep desire to do more for God, but never knew how to get it accomplished. Indeed, the cemeteries worldwide are among the wealthiest places on earth, because many visions, ideas and callings are now buried with those who had them and this is gravely unfortunate! (No pun intended.)

It is not God's desire for us to live not knowing whom He has created us to be and why we were placed on this earth. Neither is it His desire that we live having nothing and enduring a life of poverty in every way. In fact, quite the opposite is true. He said, *"Beloved, I pray that you prosper in all things and be in health, just as your soul prospers."* (3 John 2).

Have you ever felt like there is more to life than where you are at now? Have you been feeling a desire for more in your walk with God? Have you ever thought that where you are is not where you are supposed to be? Then you need to KNOW YOUR CALLING IN THE FIVEFOLD MINISTRY and this book will set you on your way to achieving just that!

God has commissioned Apostle Steve Lyston to play his part to bring order to the Body of Christ and edify the

Body of Christ; to identify their gifts, help them understand their gifts and callings, and bring out the true purpose of each person. This book that God has instructed him to write, will help you to begin realizing who you are in God; your true purpose in this life, and the value and purpose of the Spirit of God in your life – in all our lives!

Remember the Word of the Lord which says, *"My people are destroyed for lack of knowledge..."* Hosea 4: 6a.

God is stirring the gifts, talents and callings within you – that is why this book is in your hand! He is stirring up your zeal for Him, and He is calling you into a deeper, more meaningful relationship with Him. He is ready to reveal to you the "more" that you have been searching for all this time. That is why He has ordained that you have this book in your hand at this moment in time and in this particular place.

Get ready – because you are about to realize who you really are in God – whom God has called you to be.

God bless you.

Pastor Dr. Michelle Lyston
Senior Pastor
Restoration World Outreach Ministries Inc.

INTRODUCTION

God created us all with gifts, talents and solutions to change the world. It is critical for us to bring it forth. But in doing so, many are afraid to start small, when we are told not to forsake or despise small beginnings. Fulfilling God's purpose is the only way we will experience real joy.

There are many today who truly don't know their calling and are often going from here to there trying to "find" him/herself. Some are functioning outside of their calling and are going around in circles trying to make it all work. A man who does not know who he is, nor what spiritual resources he possesses will never lay hold of the level of peace and dominion for which God created them.

Knowing your calling is the first step fulfilling your purpose, and the Word of God is the key to understanding the roles and functions of doing just that.

Chapter 1

WHAT IS THE FIVEFOLD MINISTRY?

Ephesians 4: 11 – 12 says,

"And He Himself gave some to be apostles, some prophets, some evangelists, and some pastors and teachers, for the equipping of the saints for the work of ministry, for the edifying of the body of Christ..."

The Fivefold Ministry gifts are Ascension Ministry Gifts as revealed in this Scripture. These are not the gifts of the Holy Spirit per se, but an extension of Christ's Headship Ministry to the Church. In fact, it is a group of five (5) different expressions of the one Christ. The primary ministry and function of these gifts are to teach, train, activate and mature the saints for the work of the ministry and for the edifying of the Body of Christ.

Therefore, the Apostles, Prophets, Evangelists, Pastors, Teachers, spoken of in this Scripture, is the Management Team of the Church, which is responsible for empowering the saints with the resources they need to do the work of the ministry.

Why Do We Need To Have This Structure?

Ephesians 4: 13 – 16

"...till we all come to the unity of the faith and of the knowledge of the Son of God, to a perfect man, to the measure of the stature of the fullness of Christ; that we should no longer be children, tossed to and fro and carried about with every wind of doctrine, by the trickery of men, in the cunning craftiness of deceitful plotting, but, speaking the truth in love, may grow up in all things into Him who is the head—Christ—from whom the whole body, joined and knit together by what every joint supplies, according to the effective working by which every part does its share, causes growth of the body for the edifying of itself in love."

What this simply means is that as a Church we are commanded by God to be effective, and that to do so, means that we must embrace the Fivefold Ministry.

By embracing and obeying God's word, we will have:

    1) Progress in maturity (vs. 13)

2) Stability (vs. 14)
3) Integrity (vs. 15)

taking place in every individual member of the Body of Christ!

We will also experience results in the whole Body's growth, edifying, numerical expansions and internal strengthening.

Many churches only have and acknowledge the Pastors, Evangelists and maybe Teachers – Sunday School Teachers. There are even fewer churches that accept Prophets (though not altogether); but not Apostles. Apostles are not so easily understood, neither are they readily accepted – possibly because the Church generally, believes that only the Twelve that walked with our Lord Jesus were Apostles!

However, the Body of Christ and those who have been placed in charge of the sheep must understand that God is the same yesterday, today and forever, and the same principle that applied then, applies today/now! When the Body disregards the Apostles and Prophets – automatically two (2) key members of the Body are missing! If any member of a Body is missing it means that the Body will not function effectively, if at all. Just imagine that your head and neck are missing; what would happen to the rest of you? Well, remember that the

Church is likened to the Body, so if a member is missing, then you know what will happen.

Ephesians 4: 13 clearly reminds us that it is the responsibility of the Apostles and Prophets to bring the church to the fullness of Christ. Any leader that refuses to embrace the Fivefold Ministry is "anti-Anointing". This means that he/she believes in some aspects of this ministry, but refuses to embrace other parts – the Apostolic and the Prophetic, for example – and such division forces away the Anointing of God and the move of the Holy Spirit in his/her life and also in the lives of all those over whom God has given him/her charge.

In addition to this, it also means that the spirit of the anti-Christ has taken possession of him/her and his/her thoughts. Let us look at some interesting facts and see.

We must remember that God emphasizes and re-emphasizes on what He wants us to adhere to and to live by. How do you justify that based on the contents of the Bible, particularly from the original Hebrew text:

1) The term *Apostle* is mentioned 83 times

2) The term *Prophet* is mentioned 172 times

3) The term *Teacher* is mentioned 13 times

4) The term *Evangelist* is mentioned 3 times, and,

5) The term *Pastor* is mentioned only 1 time.

Think about this, generally, things are repeated for emphasis. What does this say therefore about where the emphasis is or should be placed? Think about it.

Chapter 2

THE JOEL 2 OUTPOURING

Joel 2: 28 – 29

"And it shall come to pass afterward that I will pour out My Spirit on all flesh; your sons and your daughters shall prophesy, your old men shall dream dreams, your young men shall see visions. And also on My menservants and on My maidservants I will pour out My Spirit in those days."

It is the out-pouring for all of us as stated in Joel 2, and it is time for you to know your place according to God's calling on your life within the Fivefold Ministry – without fear of the devil. It does not matter which church or congregation you are a part of, you can light the fire wherever you are. (I Corinthians 12: 28).

The Worldwide Shift That is Taking Place

God is moving man-made traditions from the church and is depending on you to take up the challenge and fulfill your calling. It is not about how long you have been in church, but about your willingness and determination to do His work. God is not looking at years of service, He is looking at your heart. (Remember Matthew 19: 30 and Matthew 20: 16)

God wants to manifest the supernatural Grace, Gifts and Power and so, the one-man-show is coming to an end. It will no longer be "a mighty man" but "a mighty Church". The ordinary Church life is over, the out-pouring of the Holy Spirit is upon all denominations, and the people around the world are feeling this stir in their spirits, so they are restless and seek more from God!

The One-Man Syndrome

God does not call one man to operate within the Fivefold ministry or other churches. Every single person within the church must be equipped for the work of the ministry as each person has different gifts and talents for the Body of Christ to function effectively.

The Fivefold Ministry is the Management Structure. The membership is the group to be equipped to do the work of the ministry.

Remember that the Spiritual Gifts and the Holy Ghost is for all. (Read - 1 Corinthians 12; Joel 2: 28 – 30; Acts 2: 38 – 39; Acts 10: 43 – 48; Mark 16: 15 – 18).

Jesus is depending on you to reap the harvest, not just the deacons and pastors – Joel 2; Luke 10: 1 – 20. As Christians, one of your functions is to be a "Salesman for Christ". The days of the Committee-run Churches are over! Contrary to popular belief, it is not who man ordains that can function in a certain capacity; but it is who God has ordained to do what He desires them to do or to have, or to accomplish!

What God Wants To Do With The Churches Now

God wants to put people in their proper offices. These offices are determined by the gifts He gives us. So, it is the responsibility, therefore, of the Leaders of the Church to make its members aware of their gifts and calling. However, many Christians are not aware of the many gifts God gives to His people, and even more so, many Christians are not aware that God is a Triune (Three-In-One) Gift-giver.

People need to know who they are in the Body of Christ; they need to know their functions in order to edify and build the Church of God.

The Triune Gift-Giver

As God is Three-In-One, He gives us gifts accordingly.

God, The Father   **Romans 12: 3 – 8**

Ministry Gifts:

1) Teaching
2) Leadership
3) Mercy
4) Exhortation

God, The Son   **Ephesians 4: 11**

Ascension Gifts:

1) Apostles
2) Prophet
3) Evangelist
4) Pastor
5) Teacher

God, The Holy Spirit   **1 Corinthians 12: 8, 10, 28**

Spiritual Gifts:

1) Word of Wisdom
2) Word of Knowledge
3) Faith
4) Healing

          5) Working of Miracles
          6) Discerning of spirits
          7) Diverse Tongues
          8) Interpretation of Tongues
          9) Prophecy

All these gifts are given for the equipping of the saints for the work of ministry for the edifying of the Body of Christ.

Chapter 3

THE GIFTS EXPLAINED

Gifts From The Father

Teaching

1) It is the supernatural ability to explain and apply the truths received from God for the Church.

2) Illustrates the Spirit's illumination providing the ability to make divine truth clear to the people of God.

3) Considered distinct from the word of the Prophet who speaks as the direct mouth piece of God.

Please note that the gift of Teaching comes in many varieties. For example, some can *teach* children, others *teach* adults. Some *teach* through writing, some through the medium of preaching, some through music, some through drama.

Leadership

1) Refers to one standing in front.

2) Involves the exercise of the Holy Spirit in modeling, superintending, and developing the Body of Christ.

3) Should be exercised with diligence.

4) It is the special ability that God gives to certain members of the Body of Christ, to set goals in accordance with God's purpose for the future – and to communicate these goals to others in such a way that they voluntarily and harmoniously work together to accomplish those goals for the Glory of God.

Mercy [Help; Service]:

1) To feel sympathy concerning the misery of another

2) To relate to others with empathy, respect and honesty

3) To be effective, this gift is to be exercised with kindness and cheerfulness, not as a matter of duty.

Recognize that the Gift of Help or Mercy is the special ability that God gives to some members of the Body of Christ to invest the talent they have in the life and ministry of other members of the Body, thus enabling the person helped to increase the effectiveness of his/her Spiritual Gifts.

Service is the special ability that God gives to certain members of the Body of Christ to identify the unmet needs involved in a task related to God's work and make use of available resources – to meet those needs and help accomplish the desired goal(s).

Exhortation [Giving]

Those who have this capacity love God deeply and give because they genuinely like to see people happy.

1) It literally means to call aside for the purpose of making an appeal

2) To entreat comfort or instruct (Acts 4: 36 / Heb. 10: 25)

3) This gift is to be exercised without outward show or pride and with liberality. (2 Corinthians 1: 12 & 8: 2, 9, 11, 13)

Giving should be done out of a spirit of generosity. Giving here refers to the action of those who have resources extending it to aid those without such resources.

Gifts From The Son

Apostle: One Sent By God

This is the special ability that God gives to certain members of the Body of Christ, to assume and exercise general leadership over a number of churches with extraordinary authority in Spiritual matters that is spontaneously recognized and appreciated by those churches.

An Apostle:

1) Is a builder, functioning much like a contractor on a construction site. They wear the helmet and carry the building plan and blueprints.

2) Deals with the strategies and tactics.

3) Functions as a messenger, a spokesman of God.

4) Implies the exercise of a distinct representative role of broader leadership given by Christ.

An Apostle must be sold out for Jesus Christ and cannot compromise concerning the truth.

In contemporary times, we refer to those who have the spirit of Apostleship in remarkably extending the work of the church – opening fields to the Gospel and overseeing large groups within the Body of Christ Jesus.
In apostolic days, they refer to a select group chosen to carry out directly the ministry of Christ including the assigned task given to a few to complete the sacred canon of the Holy Scriptures.

God's Requirements of the Apostle

1) They bring order to the Body of Christ – structure, reformation and unity – and by extension to the Nations (1 and 2 Corinthians)

2) They are foundation builders (Ephesians 2: 20)

3) They are spiritual fathers to many (1 Corinthians 4: 15) and they father churches/ministries (2 Corinthians 11: 28)

4) They walk in the Governmental Anointing/Revelation Knowledge (Ephesians 3: 5)

5) They appoint, ordain, and release divine impartation upon leaders. (Acts 6: 6)

Prophet: A Person Who Speaks From The Heart Of God – Warning, Rebuking, Instructing.

1) A Spiritually mature spokesman/proclaimer with a special, divinely focused message to the church.

2) A person uniquely gifted at times with insight into future events.

In addition to this, Prophets are:

1) Foundation builders (Ephesians 2: 20)

2) Watchmen (Jeremiah 1; Isaiah 21; Ezekiel 3; Ezekiel 33)

3) Advisors without compromise, of Kings, Businessmen, Churches and Nations (1 Samuel 9)

God's Requirements of the Prophet

1) Prophets must be persons of great integrity and must not take bribes – Jeremiah 23 and Numbers 22.

2) They must walk in the Fruit of the Spirit according to Matthew 7: 15 – 20 and Galatians 5)

3) They must be under authority – A TRUE PROPHET OF GOD MUST NOT BE A LOOSE

CANNON. They must submit to an Apostle for stability, covering and guidance.

4) They must watch the Apostle's back, as in the day of Nehemiah when he was rebuilding the wall, and blow the trumpet when the enemy is coming, not join with the enemy. (Read all the Scriptures in the Book of Nehemiah)

Evangelist: One Who Wins Souls For God

1. It is the special ability that God gives to certain members of the Body of Christ to share the gospel with an unbeliever in such a way that men and women become Jesus' disciples and responsible members of the Body of Christ.

2. The Gift of Evangelist operates for the establishment of new work. Further to this, an Evangelist can either be:

    i. Man or Woman
    ii. Lay Person or Professional
    iii. Ordained or Un-ordained
    iv. Full-Time or Part-time
    v. Personal or Public
    vi. Denominational or Inter-denominational
    vii. Mono-cultural or Cross-cultural
    viii. Serving existing churches or Planning new churches

God's Requirements of the Evangelist

1) They must preach the Word in season and out of season (1 Timothy 4)

2) They must walk in the supernatural and win the lost at any cost and the gifts of Healing and Deliverance must be manifesting in their ministry. (Acts 8)

3) They must be able to preach and teach to a wide cross-section of persons. The four (4) Gospels exemplified this through Christ's ministry while on earth

4) They must be wise and tactical in order to win souls. (Proverbs 11: 30)

Pastor: *Means To Protect – From Which We Get The* **Word**
  Shepherd

1. Implies the function of a shepherd, leader to nurture, teach and care for the Spiritual need(s) of the Body of Christ.

2. Developing unity, helping people find their gifts and doing whatever else is necessary to see that they continue in the faith and grow in their Spiritual lives.

3. The person in the office of a Pastor needs that specific gift in order to pastor. Further to this, many men and women who have the gift to Pastor/Shepherd are not functioning in that capacity because they have been placed in a different position on the Church Staff.

Recognize that Preaching has not been listed as a Spiritual gift. People who have the gift of Pastor will not necessarily be accomplished preachers - although preachers tend to draw the attention of others to themselves, Pastors tend to pour out their attention on others.

God's Requirements of the Pastor

1) They must not be irresponsible and abuse the sheep as those in Ezekiel 34: 1 – 10 and Zechariah 11: 16

2) They must not be a hireling as is explained in John 10: 12 – 13

3) They must love and care for the flock

4) They must not be manipulative and controlling

5) They must not be full of pride and too busy for the saints

Warnings for Pastors

1) Guard against the spirits of Jezebel and Ahab

2) Do not instigate or encourage disunity among the (entire) Body of Christ (Proverbs 6: 12 – 19); it goes against the Word according to John 17: 20 – 26

3) Don't compromise the truth of God for popularity

Teacher: **The One Who Instructs On The Truth Of God**

A teacher in the Fivefold Ministry is an Instructor of Truth. A teacher does not automatically carry pastoral duties. The Word of God reminds us that ***"All scripture is given by inspiration of God and is profitable for doctrine, for reproof, for correction, for instruction in righteousness"*** (2 Timothy 3: 16).

A Fivefold Ministry Teacher is one who not only teaches the Word, but also:

1) Ministers Divine Life and Holy Spirit Anointing (2 Corinthians 3: 6) and,

2) Has sharp Spiritual discernment and supernatural insight into the Word of God and how it applies to a person's daily life.

God's Requirements of the Teacher

1. They must Read, Study and Know the Word of God and spend time in His Presence.

2. They must reject heresy, corruption and falsehoods

3. They must teach the true Word of God at all times

4. They must live a Biblically-sound and holy lifestyle

5. They should never be afraid to rebuke when there is error or heresy creeping into the Church.

Gifts From The Holy Spirit

The gifts from the Holy Spirit can be further divided into three distinct groups of Gifts.

1. **Illuminative**		Word of Wisdom Word of Knowledge Discerning of spirits
2. **Oral**		Gift of Diverse Tongues Interpretation of Tongues Prophecy
3. **Dominative**		Faith Healing Working of Miracles

(*See the Gifts of the Holy Spirit Reference Guide pages 34-36*)

Recognize that God is putting His Church in order, and so you must now ask yourself the questions:

    a. What is my calling in the Fivefold?

    b. What office am I hiding under to which God did not call me?

For anyone to be effective in Ministry, he/she needs to walk in his/her calling. God wants us as the Body to function with all five (5) fingers, not just three (3).

THE GIFTS OF THE HOLY SPIRIT REFERENCE GUIDE

CATEGORY	NAME	EXPLANATION
ILLUMINATIVE GIFTS	Word of Wisdom	The supernatural perspective to ascertain the Divine means for accomplishing God's will in a given situation. Divinely given power to appropriate Spiritual intuition in problem-solving. Sense of Divine direction. Being led by the Holy Spirit to act appropriately in a given set of cirumstances. Knowledge rightly applied. Wisdom works interactively with knowledge and discernment.
	Word of Knowledge	A supernatural revelation of the Divine will and plan; Supernatural insight and understanding of circmstances or of a body of facts by revelation that is without assistance of any human resource but solely by Divine aid. Implies a deeper and more advanced understanding of the communicated acts of God. Involves moral wisdom right living in relationships. Requires object understanding concerning Divine things in human duties. May also refer to knowledge of God or of the things that belong to God as related in the Gospel.
	Discerning of Spirits	This is the special ability that God gives to some members of the Body of Christ to know with assurance whether certain types of behavior purported to be of God is in reality Divine, human or satanic. Supernatural power to detect the realm of the spirit and its activity. Implies the power of Spiritual insight, supernatural revelation of the enemy and his forces.

CATEGORY	NAME	EXPLANATION
ORAL GIFTS	**Diverse Tongues**	It is a special ability that God gives to certain members of the Body of Christ to speak to God in a language they have never learnt and/or to receive and communicate an immediate message of God to His people through a Divinely anointed utterance in a language they never learned. It enables our spirit to communicate directly with God above and beyond the power of our mind to understand. Diverse Tongues liberate the Spirit of God within us. Diverse Tongues enable the spirit of a person to take its place of ascendancy over soul and body. Diverse Tongues meet our needs for a whole new language for worship, prayer and praise.
	Interpretation of Tongues	A supernatural power to reveal the meaning of Tongues. Function not as an operation of the mind of man, but as the mind of the Holy Spirit. It does not serve as a translation (An Interpreter never understands the Tongues he/she is interpreting, but rather, gives declaration of meaning. His exercise is an miraculous and supernatural phenomenon as are the gifts of Speaking in Tongues and the Gift of Prophecy.
	Prophecy	Divinely inspired and anointed utterance. Supernatural proclamation in a known language. Manifestation of the Spirit of God, not of intellect (1 Corinthias 12: 7) May be possessed and operated by all who have the infilling of the Holy Spirit (1 Corinthians 14: 31). Intellect, Faith and Will are operative in this gift, but its exercise is not intellectually based. It is calling forth Word from the Spirit of God.

CATEGORY	NAME	EXPLANATION
DOMINATIVE GIFTS	Faith	This is a special ability that God gives some members of the Body of Christ, to discern with extra-ordinary confidence, the will and purpose of God for the future of His work. The supernatual ability to believe God without doubt, to combat unbelief, meet adverse circumstances with trust in God's message and words. Inner conviction impelled by an urgent and higher calling.
	Healing	The gift of Healing is the special ability that God gives to certain members of the Body of Christ to serve as human intermediaries through whom it pleases God to cure illness and restore health apart from the use of natural means. Refers to supernatural healing without human aid. May include Divinely assisted application of human instrumentation and medical means of treatment. Does not discout the use of God's creative gifts.
	Working of Miracles	This is a special ability that God gives to certain members of the Body of Christ, to serve as human intermediaries through whom it pleases God to perform powerful acts that are perceived by observer to have altered ordinary course of nature. Supernatural power to intervene and counteract earthly and evil forces. It literally means a display of power giving the ability to go beyond the natural. Operates closely with the gifts of Faith and Healing, to bring authority over sin, Satan, sickness and the binding forces of this age.

Chapter 4

UNDERSTANDING THE INFILLING OF THE HOLY SPIRIT AND SPEAKING IN TONGUES

As believers in Jesus Christ, we must understand that we need to accept and embrace the entire Word of God, not just parts of it. Many believe in the various gifts of God but refuse to embrace or accept the gift of Diverse Tongues. Hence, for them, speaking in tongues is a huge NO-NO! But let us also understand that this is as a result of a lack of knowledge of the Word of God and a lack of the revelation and knowledge, which comes from God through His Word and His voice.

There are many people – believers and non-believers – who, because of a lack of knowledge, fail to read and understand the Bible. They therefore tend to mock the works of the Holy Spirit and Speaking in Tongues. Please take heed therefore, to Matthew 12: 31 – 32 and Mark 3: 28 – 29. Matthew 12: 31 – 32 specifically states:

"Therefore I say to you, every sin and blasphemy will be forgiven men, but the blasphemy against the Spirit will not be forgiven men. 32 Anyone who speaks a word against the Son of Man, it will be forgiven him; but whoever speaks against the Holy Spirit, it will not be forgiven him, either in this age or in the age to come."

Prophecy and Tongues

Many persons who read 1 Corinthians 14 fail to understand this passage. Paul was specifically talking about Order in the Church – how we must conduct ourselves concerning Speaking in Tongues, Prophesying and Women's Conduct in Church. Some persons select parts of scripture, and then twist it through their own understanding to suit their immediate circumstance. They do not examine the entire scripture to get a proper understanding. This scripture is a prime example of that.

Satan has been able over the years to manipulate this scripture in order to hinder or prevent Christians from being filled with the Holy Spirit and Speaking in Tongues. By doing so, Christians are therefore less powerful than they could and should be, and they will not know or understand how to receive the Anointing from God so He can use them for signs and wonders.

Jesus Christ was crucified to give us this gift of God. Satan knows this, so he deceives the Christians and discourages them from Speaking in Tongues.

Further Understanding 1 Corinthians 14

1 Corinthians 14 speaks in greater depth of the Gift of Prophecy, Speaking in Tongues and Maintaining Order in the Church meetings when these gifts are in operation.

Let us examine 1 Corinthians 14: 2 which says,

"For he who speaks in a tongue does not speak to men but to God, for no one understands him; however, in the spirit he speaks mysteries."

Praying in an unknown tongue is a gift of the Holy Spirit. It is your spirit praying so that you can miss tragedy, gain financial blessing, and breakthrough (to name a few). This will prevent the devil from understanding what you are praying to God about, hence, we must remember that the devil cannot stop what he cannot understand. When we pray in our native language, the devil hears and understands and as a result blocks our breakthrough and answers from God, just as He did with Daniel.

If I am speaking to God privately in my heavenly language, why would anyone else need to know what I am saying to God and what He is saying to me? I am speaking to God, not man. Why would someone else need to hear when we pray or speak to God in tongues? When we speak in tongues to God, He reveals mysteries to our spirits. He breaks down walls and barriers in the Spirit, which cannot be accomplished otherwise – because we have a direct, unhindered, Divinely protected connection with God. Now you know why Satan does not want you to be filled with the Holy Spirit with the evidence of speaking in tongues.

1 Corinthians 14: 13 – 14 says,

"Therefore let him who speaks in a tongue pray that he may interpret. For if I pray in a tongue, my spirit prays, but my understanding is unfruitful."

The Bible tells us that the spirit of a man shall sustain all of his infirmities. Proverbs 18: 14 speaks of the *"...spirit in a man...".* Job 32: 8 says *"But there is a spirit in man, And the breath of the Almighty gives him understanding."*

Our spirit is the breath of God Himself. Did you know that you can get Spiritual revelations that will allow your spirit to operate your prayer life in such a way that it bypasses your intellect? The Holy Spirit will then reveal to your spirit what to pray so you can avert the tragedy before it gets to you or your family.

1 Corinthians 14: 3 – 4 tells us,

"But he who prophesies speaks edification and exhortation and comfort to men. He who speaks in a tongue edifies himself, but he who prophesies edifies the church."

Paul was comparing Speaking in Tongues with Prophecy in church services for edification and exhortation to comfort men.

1 Corinthians 14: 5 says,

"I wish you all spoke with tongues, but even more that you prophesied; for he who prophesies is greater than he who speaks with tongues, unless indeed he interprets, that the church may receive edification."

Paul's endorsement of Prophecy over tongues in corporate gatherings is qualified by equating the value of tongues with Prophecy. Therefore, Tongues without Interpretation, or for personal edification in a corporate setting will not minister to or edify the congregation. Therefore, the reverse is true – that Prophecy and Tongues with Interpretation within the congregation will minister to the entire gathering – all will understand.

Tongues may be manifested in private or public; in personal devotion or in corporate gathering. Please note that God speaks prophecies and sends messages in tongues to the church – which is why you will need someone in that gathering to interpret the message.

In 1 Corinthians 14: 6 – 13, which says,

"But now, brethren, if I come to you speaking with tongues, what shall I profit you unless I speak to you either by revelation, by knowledge, by prophesying, or by teaching? Even things without life, whether flute or harp, when they make a sound, unless they make a distinction in the sounds, how will it be known what is piped or played? For if the trumpet makes an uncertain sound, who will prepare for battle? So likewise you, unless you utter by the tongue words easy to understand, how will it be known what is spoken? For you will be speaking into the air. There are, it may be, so many kinds of languages in the world, and none of them is without significance. Therefore, if I do not know the meaning of the language, I shall be a foreigner to him who speaks, and he who speaks will be a foreigner to me. Even so you, since you are zealous for spiritual gifts, let it be for the edification of the church that you seek to excel. Therefore let him who speaks in a tongue pray that he may interpret."

Paul is saying, Prophecy is preferred above Tongues in public, where clear understanding by the hearers is the goal. Paul **did not** tell us that we must not speak in Tongues. He was teaching the church about Order. If you look at 1 Corinthians 14: 18 – 19, it says,

"I thank my God I speak with tongues more than you all; yet in the church I would rather speak five words with my understanding, that I may teach others also, than ten thousand words in a tongue."

Paul did not depreciate Tongues as a lesser gift, but thanked God for the self-edification afforded by the full measure of the gift of his own devotional life. Further to this, Paul wrote in 1 Corinthians 14: 5

"I wish you all spoke in tongues..."

In 1 Corinthians 14: 21 – 22, it says,

"Brethren, do not be children in understanding; however, in malice be babes, but in understanding be mature. In the law it is written: "With men of other tongues and other lips I will speak to this people; And yet, for all that, they will not hear Me," says the Lord. Therefore tongues are for a sign, not to those who believe but to unbelievers; but prophesying is not for unbelievers but for those who believe. Therefore if the whole church comes together in one place, and all speak with tongues, and there come in those who are uninformed or unbelievers, will they not say that you are [f]out of your mind? But if all prophesy, and an unbeliever or an uninformed person comes in, he is convinced by all, he is convicted by all. And thus the secrets of his heart are revealed; and so, falling down on his face, he will worship God and report that God is truly among you."

Paul was saying here that Tongues was also a sign for unbelievers. (See also Isaiah 28: 11 – 12; John 10: 34)

If that is the case, and all Christians are believers, then why don't some Christians believe in the Speaking of

Tongues? Examine yourself. Are you are believer or a non-believer?

According to 1 Corinthians 14: 21 – 22 which says,

"In the law it is written: "With men of other tongues and other lips I will speak to this people; And yet, for all that, they will not hear Me," says the Lord. Therefore tongues are for a sign, not to those who believe but to unbelievers; but prophesying is not for unbelievers but for those who believe."

Prophesying is not for unbelievers, but to those who believe.

In 1 Corinthians 14: 23 – 25, Paul was again speaking about Conduct in Church. If the whole church speaks in tongues at the same time, in the presence of unbelievers or the unsaved, they would not understand what we are saying. For we are speaking to God, so they might be confused or for lack of understanding say that we are mad or drunk. If the church was filled with believers only, would we call each other crazy? No! So Paul was referring to the Church, telling us that when unbelievers, the unsaved or uniformed persons come into our midst, we must prophesy to them instead. (Re-read 1 Corinthians 14: 24).

In 1 Corinthians 14: 26 – 40, Paul teaches us how to have order in church meetings. In verses 26 – 27, he tells us that when we come together, if anyone speaks in tongues in church meetings, then it should not be more than two or at most three at a time. He also speaks about prophetic utterance, that it should not go unjudged.

In 1 Corinthians 14: 28, which says,

"But if there is no interpreter, let him keep silent in church, and let him speak to himself and to God."

He tells us about interpreting if there is a message; but also that if there is no interpreter, then they must keep silent in the church. He never said not at home or in our car or in your closet. He was speaking about a church gathering. He did not say we must not speak at all, but silently let him speak to himself and to God.

Apostle Paul also tells us how prophets must speak and how others must judge in 1 Corinthians 14: 29 which says,

"Let two or three prophets speak, and let the others judge."

In 1 Corinthians 14: 30 – 33 which says,

"But if anything is revealed to another who sits by, let the first keep silent. For you can all prophesy one by one, that all may learn and all may be encouraged. And the spirits of the prophets are subject to the prophets. For God is not the author of confusion but of peace, as in all the churches of the saints."

Paul tells us again how to conduct ourselves in service – *"for God is not the author of confusion but of peace, as in all the churches of the saints."* He did not say that some, but **all** the churches of the saints. Neither did he say that some churches should speak in tongues and others should not – he was speaking about order in the churches.

In 1 Corinthians 14: 34 – 40 it says,

"Let your women keep silent in the churches, for they are not permitted to speak; but they are to be submissive, as the law also says. And if they want to learn something, let them ask their own husbands at home; for it is shameful for women to speak in church. Or did the word of God come originally from you? Or was it you only that it reached? If anyone thinks himself to be a prophet or spiritual, let him acknowledge that the things which I write to you are the commandments of the Lord. But if anyone is ignorant, let him be ignorant. Therefore, brethren, desire earnestly to prophesy, and do not forbid to speak with tongues. Let all things be done decently and in order."

Here, Paul also tells us about women, how they must conduct themselves in church. He did not say that women must not preach nor teach, nor pastor a church. In those days, women were not afforded the level of education men were. Hence, in an effort to fully understand what was being taught in the service, they would ask a lot of questions during the teaching – thus it became very noisy. So, Paul told them that they must be submissive, as the law says: "Keep silent in church" and that they should ask their husband at home.

Many churches misunderstand this particular passage of Scripture and forbid women from speaking or leading in church. You will see in 1 Corinthians 14: 39 what Paul says. He did not say we should not speak in tongues, he says,

"Therefore, brethren, desire earnestly to prophesy, and do not forbid to speak with tongues."

That is self-explanatory.

Now, therefore, let us do as Paul says in 1 Corinthians 14: 40,

"Let all things be done decently and in order."

Always remember that having Jesus as your personal Savior prepares you to live in Heaven, but receiving the in-filling of the Holy Ghost equips you with power to live every day on earth.

For your own edification, read the Word of God daily. The following Scriptures in particular will indeed open your eyes.

Matthew 10: 7 – 11 (esp. vs. 8)   Mark 16 (Read carefully)

Luke 10: 19   Luke 11: 9 – 13

Luke 24: 49   John 16: 13

Acts 1: 4 – 8 (esp. vs. 8)   Acts 2: 4 – 5

Acts 2: 17 – 18 (Joel 2: 28-30)   Acts 2: 38 – 39 (it is for *all*)

Acts 4: 5 – 10   Acts 4: 31

Acts 6: 3 – 8   Acts 7: 48 – 52 (esp. vs. 51)

Acts 7: 55   Acts 8: 10 – 22 (esp. 13, 17)

Acts 10: 43 – 47   Acts 13: 52

Romans 8: 26 – 27   Galatians 3: 1 – 5

Galatians 4: 10   Ephesians 5: 17 – 18

Ephesians 6: 18   1 Thessalonians 1: 19 – 20

Hebrews 5: 1 – 4   Jude 1: 17 – 20

So, as Luke 11: 9 – 13 says,

"…I say to you, ask and it will be given to you; seek and you will find; knock and it will opened to you. For everyone who asks, receives; and he who seeks finds; and to whim who

knocks it will be opened. If a son asks for bread from any father among you, will he give him a stone: or if he asks for a fish, will he give him a serpent instead of a fish? Or if he asks for an egg, will he offer him a scorpion? If you then, being evil, know how to give good gifts to your children, how much more will your heavenly Father give the Holy Spirit to those who ask Him?"

Acts 7: 51 says,

"You stiff-necked and uncircumcised in heart and ears! You always resist the Holy Spirit as your fathers did, so do you."

Don't let this be you. Read the Word of God for yourself and as you do, ask Him to reveal His word to you. Without knowledge you will perish! Make a change now and walk in the will of God for your life! Walk in your calling!

Chapter 5

WHO IS AN APOSTLE?

A true Apostle must possess the gift of an Apostle. This is a gift that is given by Jesus Himself. (Ephesians 4:8 – 11). It was the gift which was imparted by the Holy Spirit on the day of Pentecost (Acts 2).

The Apostle receives his gift and office by God the Father, then the entire Trinity approve. (1 Corinthians 1:1; 1 Corinthians 12:18; Ephesians 1:1). It is a sovereign decision, not an office man selects to walk in, and this is exemplified in Colossians 1:1, where Paul the Apostle, of Jesus Christ, by the will of God.

Apostles have to be eyewitnesses of the resurrected Lord. (Acts 1:22; 1 Corinthians 9:1.) In other words, an Apostle must have had a personal encounter with Jesus Christ to the point where, by way of a dream or vision, they have seen Jesus Christ face to face. I remember receiving my calling as an Apostle, I saw Jesus face to face in several visions. In one vision, He placed His nail-pierced hand on my hand. In another vision, He gave me a sword and said "Walk before Me." In seasons when we were going through great testing, Jesus appeared to me – face to face – to strengthen me or say a word of comfort. Seeing Jesus is one of the greatest encouragements one can ever receive, regardless of what one is going through.

A true Apostle, according 1 Corinthians 9: 2, 2 Corinthians 3: 1 – 6, does not need a letter of introduction and a recommendation in order to prove his legitimacy as a Minister of the Gospel; neither does that Apostle have to walk from town to town to find a pulpit from which to preach. One aspect of their genuine Apostleship must be proven by their changed life as result of the work of the Spirit in them. A true Apostle does not need man to validate them, that is done by God and exemplified in their lifestyle. Their job is to build on the Rock and bring people to Jesus Christ thus fulfilling their God-given purpose. While they are first in the hierarchy of the Fivefold ministry, they make themselves last for the building of the Kingdom of God.

The false Apostle elevates themselves, while the true Apostles are elevated by Christ. Paul trusted not in self-confidence, but confidence in the sufficiency of God's spirit. If you are a true Apostle and people lives are not being changed, something is wrong. One can be ordained as an Apostle, but is not validated or authorized by

Heaven. It means that you are illegal. (Galatians 2: 7 – 9)

As an Apostle, according to 2 Corinthians 12: 12, signs, wonders and mighty deeds will take place, but patience must accompany your ministry, and it is foremost.
Ultimately, the Apostles are the ones to gather, guide, ground, govern and send. If you are not given the grace to carry out your Apostleship, you are illegitimate and will fail. There are many who say they are Apostles and are not willing to suffer or go into difficult places and territories to establish places and individuals. Many just want a congregation that is established already to minister, but they are not willing to fulfill the Great Commission as in Matthew 28. Suffering is one of the qualifications of a true Apostle (2 Corinthians 12: 12). A true Apostle has to be called and commissioned by Jesus Christ Himself (John 20: 21). They must receive the Gospel from Christ Himself (Galatians 1:11 – 12). Not to copy a next person; they have to get a revelation of Jesus Christ, (Galatians 1:11 – 12)

True Apostles were predestined for this call before they were conceived, according to Jeremiah 1: 5 and Galatians 1: 15. Their messages come through divine revelation, not from men or traditions. Paul, the Apostle, spoke with the full backing of Jesus Christ. A True Apostle unlocks the mystery of Jesus Christ and sets the captive free. (Galatians 1: 1 – 2). Paul was not an Apostle from man, nor through man. He was an Apostle of Jesus Christ and God the Father Who raised him from the dead. Paul's

Apostolic authority was not from any human force nor through a human agency. God commissioned him. A true Apostle carries a spiritual seed of his Apostleship on the realm that cannot be duplicated or copied by man. The Apostle message must be about Jesus Christ. Paul was given his Apostolic authority directly, not from another Apostle, but from God.

Many times, the term "Apostle" is assigned qualifications according to human opinion, however, the "qualifications" of an Apostle, must be Scripturally-based. These qualifications are found only in the Word of God.

All teaching must be supported with scripture. Anything that is not supported with scripture is called Heresy. Many are walking in a Spirit of Error and under a false grace. That is why God is purging the Body of Christ. While some will have different levels of Giftings, Apostles are called and sent by God to fulfill a special mandate by God. Apostles are flexible in the hands of God, and as such can be utilized in whatever area God chooses. For example, Paul was a Pharisee, member of the Sanhedrin Council, and in fact, claims that when it came to "the Law," he was more zealous and knew more about the law than anyone else. He was of the tribe of Benjamin. Yet, he was called to the Gentiles and he edified and supported the local churches through his Teaching particularly concerning the Resurrection of Jesus Christ and His Grace. (1 Corinthians 3:6). Paul, the Apostle, also trained Timothy, Titus and others for the building, growth and development of the Church.

The difference with Paul and Apollos, is that Paul planted (churches), and Apollos "watered" them, and God gave the increase. (1 Corinthians 3: 5 – 7). God gave Paul a grace to plant/raise up churches and minister as a wise master builder. Paul laid the foundation, while Apollos watered/built on it. So, for example, not everyone has the grace to establish churches from the foundation and start it from nothing. A builder has to abide by certain builder requirements and anyone that would establish on that foundation has to abide by the principle that the foundation is built upon. They were saying in 1 Corinthians 4: 6 – 21, that Apollos was an evangelist and a teacher and not an Apostle. But Paul acknowledged him as an Apostle. A true Apostle brings structure, order, tactics and strategies. They build people, establish sound doctrine, truth. Paul was a father.

False Apostle

In the Body of Christ today, everyone wants to be first and upfront – no one wants to be a follower or function in any other gift but that of the Apostle. For some, the office of the prophet has become all too common now and so they "aspire" to become Apostle.

False Apostles are those who take on to themselves the roles of an Apostle without having been given the gift and grace to do so. They are "birthed" out of rebellion, do not submit and walk in pride. Furthermore, the are unable to trust God and so, they walk in a false Grace in order to upgrade their status.

Every office carries a grace, and if you are not given the specific grace by Jesus Christ, which is needed to effectively function in that specific capacity, then you are false, and have the potential to defile and destroy the lives of others.

We are seeing the rising of a lot of false prophets who have not been approved by God. Many are being deceived and cannot differentiate the false from the truth. Many of those functioning falsely want to start their own church and they want to lead, and not to follow. They may say they are Apostles, but of whom? They are certainly not Apostles of the Lord our God. It is for this reason that Paul, in writing to the various churches always states "Paul, the Apostle of Jesus Christ"; he is letting the Church know Who has commissioned him and Who he represents, since he encountered many false Apostles.

False Apostles focus on having titles, getting earthly accolades, having clothes, money, fame; and this is not the focus of God's true Apostles. We must recognize that a person can sit in an office, but does not have the gift or the authority that comes with it. Many of them today, purchase their credentials from social network, and many of them don't know or understand the basic tenets of

Christianity. Most of those Apostles are covering churches and are destroying many lives. Many of them take on the position of an Apostle simply because they believe it is the highest office which must automatically mean more money, more prestige, more attention, more respect and that is the position in which they think they deserve to be. Some, in order to elevate themselves even more, add secular titles. Sadly, they do this when God has not given them the grace or calling to do it and ultimately, they are not only destroying themselves and killing their true purpose, but they are in fact destroying the lives of others and killing the true purpose of others as well. Many of them do not remember what 1 Corinthians 4: 9 tells us,

"For I think that God has displayed us, the apostles, last, as men condemned to death; for we have been made a spectacle to the world, both to angels and to men."

Anyone can impersonate a law officer by wearing the uniform or a fake badge. But the question is, "Do they carry the required authority? Are they supported by Heaven? There are those who have a currency, but is their currency legally backed/supported by the nation's treasury department? If it is not, then the currency is counterfeit. In order to determine if the currency is genuine, it is tested. Banks and other organizations that deal directly with cash often test the authenticity of the bills they receive. So, every one-hundred-dollar bill is tested to determine its authenticity. It is critical for us, in these end times, to discern the true Apostles from the false Apostles. (2 Corinthians 11: 13 – 15).

Paul clearly outlines the characteristics of false Apostles and reminds us in 1 Corinthians 3: 12 – 13 says, ***"Now if anyone builds on this foundation with gold, silver, precious stones, wood, hay, straw, each one's work will become clear; for the Day will declare it, because it will be revealed by fire; and the fire will test each one's work, of what sort it is."*** So the substance of everyone's work will be tested.

Paul further reminds us that there are those who pose as angels of light, ***"And no wonder! For Satan himself transforms himself into an angel of light."*** (2 Corinthians 11: 14). Apostles of Jesus Christ are about the Kingdom and boast about their struggle or suffering. (2 Corinthians 8: 1 – 4).

The Apostle's Role As A Father

The Apostle is a father who mentors individuals and guides them into their purpose. They are responsible for disciplining you, and nurture you and your gift according to Ephesians 6: 4.

Just as our Heavenly Father does, a father has the capacity to speak life upon and within his children and impart to them as well. That is why a father must not compromise when it comes to disciplining his children. Eli failed to discipline his children and it caused the Ark of the Covenant to be captured. Samuel also failed to discipline his sons in 1 Samuel 8: 3 - 6. True fathers bring correction to their household and bring their children in line. When fathers fail to bring correction, their children will bring shame and disgrace.

A father also shows compassion to his children in the same way the Lord shows compassion to those who fear him. Psalms 103:13. A true son and daughter will always listen to their father. There are those people who listen only to those they like to hear, otherwise they are gone.

Lucifer fell because he didn't want to honor the Heavenly Father. He rejected the Heavenly Father's covering by His actions and instead wanted to *be* a covering. (Ezekiel 14; Ezekiel 28). He competed with the Father. Anything that is not covered becomes unclean, because it leaves you open to the elements without a filter. When one rejects earthly fathers, they are in fact, symbolically rejecting the Heavenly Father. Your earthly father is your covering not your pal/friend. Your father is your father. Your friend will tell you what you want to hear, but your father will tell you what you *need to* hear but don't want to hear. The things that you don't want to hear are often the things that will bring you great blessing.

A father teaches his children:

1. To respect authority, whether spiritual or physical authority. (Proverbs 4:1 – 9).

2. Truth, and how to respect God's word. A person will never get wisdom unless they listen to the instruction of their father.
3. Good, sound doctrine. Solomon received the doctrine of the law from David. Part of his wisdom came from what David had taught him. If he didn't listen to his father, the Holy Spirit would never have stayed around them.

If a person is unwilling to submit, they will not be able to receive wisdom from their father's teaching. (Proverbs 13: 24). Proverbs 13: 18 also tells us that if a person refuses instruction, spiritual and natural poverty will come upon them. We must follow instructions given by God's word. Obedience brings blessings.

The word "Father" simply means "a male parent, a person who founds a line or family." It also means "a man who starts, creates, or invents something." God, the Father – Who created man is our example of who a father should be; hence our prayer in Matthew 6. The man, especially in his capacity as a father, is the symbol of the Heavenly Father as we are made in His image; and this is the main reason there are so many attacks against the fathers. Remember that the devil hates the Heavenly Father. Sadly, many laws have been passed over the decades that target or marginalize fathers.

Proverbs 13: 6 reminds us

"a wise son heeds his father's instruction, but a scoffer does not listen to rebuke"

and they will continue in their evil ways. A true father, according to Deuteronomy 6: 6 – 9, teaches his children about God's goodness when they sit in their house, when they walk by the way, when they lie down and when they rise up. The Word of God must be the criteria for all things. We must teach our children, now more than ever, how to honor a father whether it is our biological father, stepfather or our Heavenly Father.

God is looking for true sons and daughters so the Holy Spirit can dwell/reside within them. The breakdown within our society and within the Church is as a result of the breakdown of good parenting and a sore lack of disciplining. Today, sons and daughters are free to carry out any act of indiscipline; and if they are disciplined, they rebel. Ultimately, it has the potential to terminate their true purpose. Hebrew 12: 7 – 11 clearly states that anyone who does not get disciplined are illegitimate children.

True sons and daughters:

1. Care about their spiritual and physical parents.

2. Know that the inheritance of the parents belongs to them, so they do not have to compete. It is theirs to tap into.

3. Will never join with others to discredit their father or the Apostle or uncover their nakedness. They always want the best for their parents.

God is raising up fathers to bring transformation to and through the family and the Body of Christ. (Mark 10:18 – 19; Luke 18: 19 – 20; Ephesians 6: 2 – 3; Colossians 3: 20; Proverbs 6: 2; Ephesians 6:1)

The Apostle And The Roles Of The Fivefold Ministry

According to Ephesians 4: 11, the Fivefold Ministry builds, equips, empowers, establishes new churches and raises up leaders. The Fivefold Ministry also:

1. Establishes unity

2. Establishes the Great Commission according to Matthew 28.

3. Brings alignment to the Family and the Church

4. Strategizes and directs the execution of those strategies during Spiritual Warfare,

5. Establishes General Prayer, 24-Hour Prayer, Counseling and Feeds the Poor.

6. Brings the Government of God on the earth.

The Fivefold ministry functions as in the Book of Acts, where the sick can be healed, there is real discipleship, leaders are established, and there is order in the Body of Christ. The Apostle is responsible for ensuring that the specifics of the Fivefold Ministry that is given to him/her by God is executed and as such fulfill their God-given mandate.

The Fivefold Ministry is the ministry of Grace. The five (5) offices form the comprehensive managerial structure for the Body of Christ, which births sons and daughters. Fivefold leaders equip, edify, and send. They also:

1. Take dominion over territories,

2. Impact different cities,

3. Focus on and cover all areas of life – spiritually and naturally.
4. Bring the saints into maturity.

Whether it be politics, entertainment, faith, education, or security, the Fivefold Ministry is the answer. Fivefold Leaders equip the saints for the work of the ministry. The gifts and talents of each and every person within a Fivefold Ministry must be utilized for the fulfillment of God's purpose in the earth.

The Fivefold Ministry is like an army; they are not regular church-goers. They demonstrate the power of God within the earth. No Fivefold Ministry should be comfortable behind the four (4) walls; they must get out in the community. There is no need to fight for or about positions within a Fivefold ministry unless you don't fully understand your role. Each person is being equipped to be sent. "To be sent" does not mean leaving the Church, but ideally it means the person(s) would be trained and placed over different regions like New York or Paris – branches within specific areas in the ministry.

The focus of a Fivefold Ministry is not on erecting a building, but on building the people. There are many churches today that are called "Fivefold" but if you take a good look at their internal structure, it mainly/only allows everybody to be in one building, instead of going out in various places to minister to the needs of the communities comprehensively. God will hold such churches accountable, and allow those churches to be sifted in the end time, and raise up willing ones functioning under the true Fivefold structure.

Fivefold Leadership Support

It is critical for each person within a Fivefold Ministry to hold up the hands of their Visionary/Apostle so that the Divine mandate can be fulfilled. In Exodus 17: 10 – 13, whenever Aaron and Hur held up/supported the hands of Moses during the battle, the children of Israel started winning. The Visionary within a Fivefold Ministry is no different. Many times, the Visionary/Apostle gets battered, so-to-speak, because of the lack of support from the people within that Fivefold vision. Sadly, most do not want to help carry the burden; they do not want to do what it takes to support the Fivefold structure, nor put in the effort it takes to be an effective team for God.

Support The Apostle And The Corporate Vision

So, keeping in mind all the things that must be accomplished by and through the Fivefold Ministry, recognize that the Visionary – the Apostle – must focus on:

1. The vision,

2. The Word,

3. Prayer and Fasting, and

4. Spiritual Warfare

to facilitate growth and expansion.

Oftentimes, because of the lack of support from within, they ultimately have to get involved in the simple, day-to-day running of the ministry. As Acts 6 tells us, the Apostles should *not* be the ones "serving tables", that is, paying rent/mortgage, bills, seeing to the distribution of food, and so on, because it negatively impacts on the church's growth and the development of the saints. This is why Deacons were selected and their role established in the Fivefold Ministry. When the Deacons are functioning as they should, then it allows the Apostle to focus on the building plan for the Church's growth and development. God gives each Apostle a dimension of how to build for which they are accountable. When your Apostle is focused on the wrong area, because of lack of support, it negatively impacts both the Apostle and the congregation.

There is too much division at times within the Fivefold ministry, because everyone wants to establish his/her own vision; not recognizing that as they establish the corporate vision, it opens the door for what God has put within them to come to fruition as well.

They should, instead, find out their role in the plan, receive their instructions by way of the Apostle and function in their assigned area. Remember, Apostles are coaches, mentors, fathers. The people within the Fivefold ministry are a team, coming together to win, similar to what we see in the NBA matches. The Team loses when everyone wants to be a star, when everyone becomes selfish and begins to focus on him/herself. These days in ministry, everyone wants to be seen, and wants to lead; very few want to follow and learn. The only Star in ministry is Jesus Christ.

When God calls you to a vision, ensure that you fulfill your assignment. Don't allow anyone or anything to pull you away from your place of assignment. Ensure that no one causes you to lose your focus or assignment. The Fivefold Ministry is a place of blessing. (Genesis 22). It is an altar of sorts, where provision is already made for you, and it is when you are connected to the vision that you will see the provision.

There are many functioning as Apostles out there who have not been called to do so; and do not have the Divine Permission nor Grace from God to function as an Apostle. We must be aware and vigilant, so that we will not be deceived.

Chapter 6

PROPHETS AND PROTOCOL

It is key within the Church and in the Fivefold Ministry, that protocol is established within the environment where the Prophetic gift manifests in order to maintain integrity. There are many people's lives that have been seriously and negatively affected because of the Prophetic Ministry of immature and rebellious individuals who do not possess the Fruit of the Spirit.

The Different Kinds of Prophets

There are two main types of Prophets: *Nabi* and *Seer*. Generally speaking, the **Nabi** is *audio* and the **Seer** is *visual*.

Nabi literally means "*to bubble up*." It describes one who is stirred up in spirit. When the sense of "bubbling up" is applied to speaking, it becomes "to declare." Hence, a Nabi, or a prophet, is an announcer—one who pours forth the declarations of God.

The category of the **Seer** is further broken down into two kinds – **Roeh** and **Hozeh**

1. ***Roeh*** means *"to see"* or *"to perceive"*. It is generally used to describe one who is a revealer of secrets, one who envisions.

2. ***Hozeh*** also means "to see" or "to perceive," but is also used in reference to musicians. It is also used to describe a counselor or an advisor to a king.

There are also different functions of Prophets within the Church. There are:

Administrative Prophets: prophets that can govern within the Fivefold Ministry, meaning they can equip, manage, impact and train; they have leadership ability. They can also write and supervise other prophets to keep them in line.

Operational Prophets: prophets, also within the churches, who warn, encourage, motivate, they also can give direction, as we see in Acts 11: 27. These prophets must be in submission - not self-serving or independent of the local assembly. They are not for entertainment as we see happening in the church now-a-days. In Acts 21: 11, Agabus gave personal prophecy to Apostle Paul. God is calling prophets to prophesy, to warn and to advise, like

Prophet Nathan in the Bible who spoke to David in 2 Samuel 12: 13. Isaiah also spoke to King Hezekiah, dealing with personal matters.

The Elijah Prophet

In Malachi 4, there are many misunderstandings of the Prophetic Ministry. The Prophetic Ministry brings solutions to global problems, healing and restoration to confront spiritual forces and the spirit of Jezebel. God is calling people to walk in the spirit of Elijah. Restoring the families, bringing economic solutions, military strategies, and being advisors for Kings, calling back the people to true worship, especially from new age philosophy. Pray to break famine and recession as we have seen Elijah and Elisha do, rebuilding altars and tear down evil altars.

Elijah, Elisha, and John the Baptist carried the same type of anointing in the Bible. They may have dressed differently and preached differently, and acted differently, were considered the misfits of society, but they were set apart. (Hebrew 11: 37). Many of them were being persecuted, beheaded, murdered, and some of them living in the wilderness. They lived a life of suffering and torment but they have never compromised the mandate. We need, according to Malachi 4, prophets like these to walk in the mantle of Elijah for an End-Time Restoration. Especially for the family. They were not afraid to wander and walk in the mountains and the wilderness. They walked by faith; they are not afraid to confront Jezebel and those who worshipped Baals.

As an Elijah prophet, you will experience isolation, discouragement and loneliness in your walk. These are the prophets that God will used to repair the broken-down altar. They are set apart and separated from the things of the world. They walk in the supernatural faith and bring back the people unto God by reestablishing their faith unto Him. There are many people calling themselves prophets, but do they truly know what being a prophet means or does. A prophet is not one who seeks profits, or seeking accolades or fame. Rather they are called by God to speak "***Thus saith the Lord…***". Their (general) purpose is to establish the Government of God as the Foundation of the Cross. If Christ is not the foundation within the Prophetic Ministry and the prophet is not leading the people of Christ, it is **counterfeit**. More attention has been given to the prophet (the messenger), than to Jesus Christ - the Sender of the message.

1. The Elijah prophet brings people to Christ and not to self. (1 Peter 1:18 – 20.) Furthermore,

2. His/Her life and messages shared must be in line with Biblical Principles. Everything a prophet does **must** be in line with the Word of God.

3. He/She must pray for the heart of the people to turn back to God.

4. He/She must be a fearless reformer, not afraid to rebuke kings, must be a mighty prayer warrior, a vessel through whom God can work miracles signs and wonders; drought breaker, high multiplier; to flow in the Ministry of resurrection and reconciliation.

The Holy Spirit fire will be on the Elijah generation. God is calling the Church back to the Cross, and for this reason, He is raising up the Elijah generation. It is this generation that will bring the people back to the Cross; that the Spirit of God will pour out into the earth, and we will experience the abundance.

The Elijah generation is about a vessel willing to be used by God, being dedicated to God. Those who have made up their minds to pay the price will likely experience persecution and isolation. God is looking for an Elijah generation who is:

1. Not afraid to be feed by raven, widow, or Angels.

2. Not afraid, in the End Times, to call down the fire of God as instructed by the Lord.

3. Always ready to serve in any direction that God wants them to serve.

God will use them to bring healing within the earth and the Gathering within the harvest. They will bring back purity and holiness to the church. Their number one focus is and will always be to glorify Jesus within the earth. If you are ready for the challenge and you are feeling a stir within your spirit, you may be of the Elijah generation.

The Prophetic Gifting Is For Doing Good

The Prophetic Gift is not to be abused at any level or used to manipulate anyone, even if the person morally falls. Unfortunately, there are many prophets who use the gift to manipulate or blackmail others for personal gain.
Each time you are receiving a prophetic word, from someone within the church and external of the church, you have the right to record that word for the purpose of accountability. Go to your shepherd/pastor for all confirmation.

There are negative views about the office of a Prophet or the Prophetic Ministry. Many have been hurt and turn away from the Prophetic because of the lack of integrity. Integrity is key within the Prophetic Ministry. We should never be fooled by accuracy to say a person is a true prophet. Jesus said, by their fruit you should know them. (Matthew 7; Galatians 5). The Fruit of the Spirit is key. Many are just seeking fame, accolade, money; because of that, they are fabricating the truth. Balaam started out as a true prophet, however, because of the pitfall in his life, he ended up becoming a false prophet. He began to divine and release curses for money.

There are many prophets will collect money to do evil. There are prophets who are covering evil wicked men such as those involved in drugs. Any prophet who gives a word for one to walk in rebellion is not of God. For example, the so-called "prophetic word" given for saved individuals to marry unsaved individuals is not of God. Words given for people to divorce their current spouses and marry someone else is not of God. Some have given false prophecies of the amount the receiver of the prophecy has in his/her bank account and has been instructed to withdraw the amount and take it in to the false prophet. Word given to walk away from the local church is not of God. Word given for you to gamble, walk in sexual impurity - all of these are not of God. There are many within the Body of Christ who have great potential, but their lives are being destroyed by prophets who are not walking in integrity.

The Bible says we should judge all prophetic utterances especially those that are key to your advancement and development. Many false prophets will tell you not to submit prophetic word to your leader, like your local Apostle or Pastor. The Prophetic Ministry is to bring you out of bondage, not to bring you into bondage. God is not in the heart of confusion. Prophets are not spokespersons for a political party, they are spokespersons from God. Many political leaders are falling away in error because of counsel they receive from the Korah (rebellious) prophet. We have seen it with the old and young prophets in the Old Testament. True prophets are part of the Foundational Ministry as found in Ephesians 2: 20. They are there to help the Apostles establish the local church, and so, must walk in sound doctrine, according to Titus 9.

Deuteronomy 13: 1 – 3 is a key scripture for individuals to read and use it as a guideline to evaluate the Prophetic Ministry. We need the Prophet and the Prophetic Ministry. Any church that does not encourage or establish the Prophetic Ministry within the congregation is a **dead** church. Pastors and Bishops must look beyond the negative things that the enemy has done to tarnish the Prophetic Ministry and begin to raise up prophets with integrity within the local church.

We must establish order, we must judge prophetic words, and teach the roles and functions of the Prophet within the prophetic church so that they – Prophets – do not become loose cannons; they must subject themselves to the elders within the local church. They are there to watch the Apostle's back while he is building.

1 Corinthians 14:1 helps us to understand that the operation of the Gift of Prophecy is for edification, exaltation, and comfort. Each believer has the ability to prophesy, to give insight, direction and confirmation. We must establish protocol within the local church for the operation of the Prophetic Gifting. (1 Corinthians 14: 31; 1 Peter 4:11; 1 Corinthians 14: 26 – 33).

We need to prophesy and give people hope, to motivate and encourage, to strengthen individuals regardless of how discouraged we are ourselves. When a prophetic word is declared, your entire life begins to transform. The Prophetic Gifting has even split many churches because of lack of supervision. The Bible says in 1 Corinthians 14: 29 "Let two or three prophets speak, and let the others judge." We need the prophetic more than ever within the End-Time.

Accountability

The Pastor of a church must have a system of accountability where all Prophetic utterances are tested in accordance with 1 Corinthians 14. This will also prevent church splits. The Pastor should have a book to log all Prophetic Words or a means of recording each prophetic utterance given. They must ensure that visitors and young converts are protected, so that no one will pull them away after service in the car park to bring defilement and confusion upon them.

Imagine that there is a vibrant new convert, filled with zeal, ready to be a part of the vision, but they need healing, deliverance and training. Then someone connects with them after service one Sunday and "prophesies" to them, telling them that they should start their own ministry. Imagine also that there is a new convert or new member who is actively serving at the church, but someone in the church connects with them, gives them a "prophetic word" telling them that God has called them (the new convert) to serve them, not the church they attend. In either instance, they begin to invite the new convert over to their house for dinner and proceed to "minister to them" prophetically. This kind of behavior can destroy a person's life and even abort their ministry; it can lead to bitterness, causing them to not want anything to do with Prophets or the Prophetic Ministry.

There are many today who have received a prophetic word that they must sell their property and relocate, only to lose everything. What is even worse is that there are some who have great potential in ministry, but receive a word to walk away from the church and from their God-given ministry, are told to resign their positions without consulting with the leader/shepherd over them. Today they are nowhere spiritually and have lost much.

Guest Speaker Protocol

Pastors must have proper protocol in place where it concerns Guest Speakers to their churches. Those Guest Speakers will connect with the members of the church they are visiting, pass out business cards or invite them to connect on social network and proceed to poison those people out of the will of God for their lives. Some go as far as sleeping with the members. Pastors, watch the fruit, not the accuracy. It is critical for Pastors to understand that for every truth, there is a fake. There are many extra virgin olive oils out there that have been mixed with other oils. There are counterfeit dollars, but a special light can be used to identify the material with which the dollar is made. There are a number of fakes within the Body of Christ that have not been validated or processed within the local church. We tend to look at accuracy and ignore the Fruit of the Spirit. Big mistake! (Galatians 5; Matthew 7).

We must ensure that there is strict protocol to govern, monitor and protect those within the local church. You must know the lifestyle they are living. Most want to be like the others they see on television. We cannot continue to be naïve concerning the things that happen. Paul said in Acts 20: 29 – 31,

"For I know this, that after my departure savage wolves will come in among you, not sparing the flock. Also, from among yourselves men will rise up, speaking perverse things, to draw away the disciples after themselves. Therefore watch, and remember that for three years I did not cease to warn everyone night and day with tears."

Protocol Checklist

There are many people moving from church to church and some are even members of church and will tell you that they have other spiritual parents separate from the leaders at their church. Remember, anything that has two heads is a monster – like Leviathan. It is not Scriptural for persons to have a local pastor or an Apostle over them while they take instructions from other places outside of their local church. In a case like that, they would never receive a double portion from their leader. God is not the author of confusion.

Remember to:

1. Record all prophecies, whether in a book, or on audio.
2. Report all prophecies you receive – personal and otherwise – to your leader.

3. Check to see if the person who gives you the prophecies, is one who is under spiritual authority, that is, someone to whom they are accountable.

4. Check the motives of the prophecies. Check to see if what you are being told will potentially pull you away from the vision you are under and toward the person giving you the prophecy.

5. Check to see if the prophetic word is scripturally sound. For example, if you are already married, and especially if you are having marital issues, and you receive a prophetic word that there is another spouse for you, that is not scripturally correct. Also, if you are a single Christian, and you are being told to marry an unsaved person, that is not scripturally sound. If you receive a prophetic word to date someone, that is not scripturally correct.

6. Ensure all important words that concern your future, for example, moving to a new location or

marriage, that prophecy must be confirmed with two or three to judge.

Remember, the focus must not be on the accuracy of the prophetic word given, or on the person giving the word, but on the Fruit of the Spirit. In other words, what is the lifestyle of the person giving the Word? Are they married? Are they walking in integrity?

True prophetic word must bring edification, exhortation and comfort. (1 Corinthians 14: 3)

If a prophecy comes to pass, and promotes disobedience against God, or Scripture, it is not a true prophecy. (Deuteronomy 13: 1 – 3). Please note that God can allow a prophetic word to come to pass, although the person releasing the word was not true.

If someone gives a word to look to other sources for help – such as a horoscope, magic, New Age sources – it is not of God. A true word brings liberty NOT manipulation or intimidation, nor should it cause you to become dependent on the person. (2 Corinthians 3: 17). Remember, a word can come to pass but does not give honor to Jesus, and instead promotes the person giving you the word. (Deuteronomy 13: 1 – 3)

Please note that Prophecy deals with the future, and it is not the same as Word of Knowledge. All the gifts can be counterfeited by Satan, so it is critical for you to know the difference. Satan is a copycat. Remember that a counterfeit dollar can do the same thing as the real dollar, but it is not legal tender and as such, the source and the counterfeit are illegal.

Accuracy

In the Bible, accuracy is critical and has the capacity to bring many to Jesus Christ. It can also bring healing to individuals and solve legal problems. However, in order for us to accurately receive and release the prophetic word from the Lord, we must follow instructions given. (Luke 5). God wants us to have the five (5) senses in the spiritual realm – see, hear, taste, smell and touch. It is critical to have that kind of sensitivity in the realm of the spirit.

In Luke 5, the fishermen were struggling; after an entire night's work they caught nothing. However, upon Jesus' instructions to launch out in the deep, they made the catch of a lifetime. Jesus knows where the fishes are – He created them.

Neither time nor season can hinder miracles. Accuracy can bring great provision, but priority must be given to the Fruit of the Spirit; because there are many who are accurate concerning the prophetic word, but beyond that, they bring reproach to the Kingdom and to the name of the Lord. Matthew 17: 24 – 27 shows us the accurate word from Jesus to Peter to get the coin from the mouth of the fish. Jesus knew the exact location of the fish, and which fish it would be. Wouldn't it be lovely if God told us exactly where to find the "fish" we need?

There are many out there with money in their mouths so-to-speak, but we need the spiritual eyes to see the exact location. (John 1: 45 – 50). We must depend on the Holy Spirit to show us the deep things. God is the Revealer of secrets. John 1: 50 says,
"Jesus answered and said to him, "Because I said to you, 'I saw you under the fig tree,' do you believe? You will see greater things than these."

Wouldn't you want to see the heavens open – angels ascending and descending? In Genesis 28: 11 – 13, Jacob saw it.

The Apostle Paul saw some things he could not explain or utter. Jesus' accuracy in John 4: 16 – 29 birthed the first evangelist to be recorded in the Bible – the woman at the well. He also saw the source of her problems and the solutions she needed.

Accuracy is needed to bring people to the Kingdom and set them free from the forces of darkness. (2 Kings 6: 8). Accuracy for intelligence gathering is needed in the end-time to see and hear the plans of the enemy. At times, a picture is greater than a word spoken. We need accuracy to save lives in the End-Time. In 2 Kings 5, accuracy brought healing to Naaman, but the prophet – Elisha – was not interested in remuneration. He did not want money. In order to have good spiritual sight, the prophet cannot be blinded by mammon. Psalm 119: 18 says,

"Open my eyes, that I may see wondrous things from Your law."

We need our eyes to be open to see revelation in the Word of God. The Lord wants us to sit at His feet so that our eyes can be opened as we see in Luke 10: 38 – 42. Many are too busy "serving" everywhere and attending to everything, all of which hinder them from seeing.

Discernment of Spirits Help You To See

The Gift of Discernment of Spirits will help you to see in the realm of the spirit, that you will be able to differentiate the natural from the supernatural, the human versus the demonic, lying spirits, wrong motives, and also help you to identify the Holy Spirit at work. (Acts 5; Acts 8: 22 – 24; Acts 13: 6 – 12; Acts 16: 16 – 18)

Taste

God uses the Spiritual senses at times to teach us and communicate with us. Ezekiel 3: 3 reminds us to "eat" the Word. You must read the Word to develop the appetite for the Word of God. Once someone gives you the wrong food, you will know it. You will know whether it is good or not. Food represents doctrine. (1

Kings 4: 38 – 41). We must discern false teachers and wrong doctrine in the End-Time. One of the sons of the prophets was not satisfied with what he was receiving in the school of the prophets, hence, he went out and ate elsewhere and became poisoned by the doctrine/food he received. There was death in the pot. Once a person gets poisoned, they tend to bring it back into their church to poison others. Most in the Prophetic Ministry walk about from ministry to ministry, and when they get poisoned, they bring it back to home base and poison others. That is why the True Prophets of God must bring them back to true doctrine, (symbolized in the Scripture by flour). This is clear according to Psalm 119: 103 – 104 and 1 Peter 2: 3.

Touch

Have you ever been touched by someone or something, and you do not feel right? Have you ever laid hands on someone as you pray for them and you do not feel right? Sometimes you go into a church service and people seem to like laying hands on you, or rest their hands on your shoulder, back or head, or on your children and something does not feel right? Physical contact – touch is very important. The wrong touch can create wrong covenants or soul ties. Be careful about who touches you, or whom you touch. Be careful of who does your hair or massages you. God wants us to touch the hem of His garment so that we can be healed and whole. (Mark 9: 21). There are many in the Fivefold Ministry who would touch us but we must know what they do, because we must guard the anointing God has given. (2 Corinthians 6: 17; Colossians 2: 21)

Sound

Sound is critical in the realm of the spirit in order to understand what God is saying and what is coming up on the land. Every great move is preceded by a sound.

1. In Exodus 32: 17 -18 when Moses was coming down from the mountain, both he and Joshua heard the same noise, but each heard a different sound in the noise. Moses heard singing, and Joshua heard the sound of war – and both knew something was not right.

2. Elijah also heard a sound and discerned that it was the sound of the abundance of rain. (1 Kings 18: 41)

3. In Jeremiah 50: 22, he heard the sound of battle in the land.

4. In Psalm 89: 15, God's people hear a joyful sound. Sound is therefore very important in the Prophetic Ministry.

Smell

Smell in the spiritual realm has to do with discernment and is very important regarding Prophetic Ministry and Spiritual Warfare.

Sometimes you may enter an environment and you know that what you are smelling is not physical. In other words, what you are smelling is not from the current physical environment. Demons can come around you and the Lord will allow you to smell them.

Sight

Sight is critical within the Body of Christ. We need eagle's eyes in order to see like an eagle. We need 20/20 vision. A person's eyes can be wide open in the natural, but they are spiritually blind, unable to discern dangers and wrong motives.

What we see happening in Mark 1: 21 – 26, is what typically happens in today's churches. Religious folks cannot discern what is in their midst and sometimes the enemy plants dangerous seeds in our midst. Some are given the authority within the church – Board Members and decision-makers. We must see beyond the natural realm before we appoint different ones in positions of authority within the church, or any organization for that matter. We must be able to identify the Jezebel,

Leviathan, and the Devil that is in our midst, and cast them out, if we are to have peace in our church.

Chapter 7

THE STRUGGLES OF A PROPHET

Many times, people will want to judge a prophet or see them as above reproach; but as prophets of God, they cannot function without the Holy Spirit. They go through problems on a daily basis in the same way everyone else does. The Holy Spirit will use them many times to bring healing and deliverance to many, but they themselves suffer with the very same things from which God uses them to deliver others. For example, prophets go through rejection too, as well as fear, loneliness, moral struggles, emotional issues, and poverty. Both Elijah and Elisha – great prophets of God – one had to be fed by a raven, the other had to endure famine. As God used them tremendously, they too had to depend on God to use others to feed or help them. Jeremiah also suffered great hardships. He was even imprisoned.

There will be times that everyone around the prophet – those to whom the prophet will minister – will receive great breakthroughs – while the prophet continues to wait on the Lord for their release, victory or breakthrough to come for them personally. This is why we depend on the anointing of the Holy Spirit which enables us and does an inner work in us.

As prophets of God, it is critical for us, if we want God to use us, to keep going deeper into the Word of God. We must also be knowledgeable of world events and how it aligns with Biblical Prophecies.

We must know/study about

1. Times and Seasons

2. Trees and how they function

3. Agriculture, so that we can harness the solutions God is revealing through these areas.

We must

1. Value our mouth,

2. Live a consecrated life

3. Believe when we speak that it will come to pass

4. Know the scope of our calling – whether we are called to the Church or to the Nations. Daniel, Nehemiah, Joseph, Ezra, Elijah and Elisha were all called to the Nations. They had the ability to govern – not just in the Church, but also in nations and in the area of politics.

King David was a musician and a prophet. Asaph was also a musical prophet whose grace allowed him to play music that changed the direction of the nation. Furthermore, they had the anointing to impact wars.

A prophet is like a policeman – God's messenger and authority within the earth. God is waiting on you to move and is looking for the word He has given you to come forth. He wants you to police the illegal activities of Satan within the earth. Some come through the media bringing destruction upon the youth and the Church. We are the ones to speak the truth when deception is taking place within the earth. The prophet must speak when the poor, the fatherless, and the widows have been mistreated, especially by the political and business persons.

There are many things happening globally and the prophets are silent. Most are simply focusing on houses, cars and that is not what the prophets ought to be about according to the Word of God.

Prophet In The Making

There is much controversy taking place in the Prophetic Ministry and many are confused about the role and function of a prophet in the Body of Christ. The office of a Prophet still exists and is still relevant today. God wants prophets, but the role and accountability in the Old Testament is different from the New Testament.

In the Old Testament, the Prophets were only accountable to God, but in the New Testament, the Prophet is accountable to the Leadership of the Church. The Leadership or Management Team of the Church consists of the Apostles, Prophets, Evangelists, Pastors, Teachers (of the Word). The Old Testament Prophet, carried doctrinal and ecclesiastical authority.

The maturing of a Prophet is not an overnight thing. They have to be tested in many areas. For example, the Word Test, the Patience Test, the Wilderness Test, the Time Test, the Pride and Submission Tests. After God used Elijah the Prophet to give word to the king, he still had to go by the Brook Cherith, for further processing! He had to undergo scarcity and be fed by the ravens! How many prophets would want to do that today?

There are five (5) Ascension Gifts Jesus gave to build the local Church according to Ephesians 4: 11. It means that the prophet alone cannot build the local church. Likewise, prophecy alone does not build the church. A sound church must have proper doctrine, must be led by the Holy Spirit and the Word and must engage in Fasting and Prayer. In the same way, the Prophet needs the other Ascension gifts for his/her development. He needs the Apostle to put order and structure in his life. He needs the Teacher to instruct him in proper doctrine/truth, and he needs the Pastor to nurture him into maturity.

A Prophet of God ought to be a spokesman for God. They must have the DNA and the image of God, as well as the Fruit of the Spirit. Their message must be in line with God's Word!

Prophets must not give a word to draw people unto themselves, they must function to direct people to God and Jesus must be center of their message! (Isaiah 51: 16). The prophet is to communicate God's mind and will in the earth! A prophet must speak the Word God puts in his mouth. He should speak all that God commands him to speak! (Deuteronomy 18: 18). He should not speak his personal word, but God's word.

A prophet's number one criteria is not to foretell the future, but to bring correction to the Church and to the nation(s) and the proclamation of moral truth. Foretelling the future accurately does not prove that they are True Prophets. Jesus outlined in Matthew 7 that by their fruit you shall know them. (Galatians 5)

The enemy is shifting the focus from Truth and the Fruit to Foretelling the future, hence, one can call himself a prophet while he lives any lifestyle he chooses – which is contrary to God's Word!

A True Prophet functions with order and is in submission. A True Prophet has no problem with either of those requirements; neither are fame and money his sole focus. Souls, Restoration and the Ministry of Reconciliation must be his main areas of focus. Encouragement, Exhortation, Intercession and the Building of the local Church must be his main activities.

Prostitution of the Anointing

There are many within the Body of Christ, because of their Laziness to seek God, are creating an atmosphere for the Prostitution of the Anointing. As a result, many prophets are now falling away because of the demands placed on them. Likewise, many churches are going through great financial problems because of a lack of faith. They have opened a door, and are now creating a monster called Prostitution.

Every prophet's message, maturity and morality are some of the keys we must use to help us discern them as prophets of God. Likewise, they must have the DNA of Jesus in them; and those within the Office of a Prophet must not fall to the temptation and become a Psychic to God's people, particularly when they have no intention to read God's Word.

Many Pastors need to repent and stop promoting this behavior as it brings reproach to Christ's Church and to Him. Some of the Pastors are more guilty than those in the office of the Prophet.

Because of the great reproach upon the Prophetic Ministry today, many are now "migrating" to the office of the Apostle. But before they consider doing so, and take on a false grace, it would be best for them to study about the life of an Apostle. It is a life of Suffering! They have to become last so that others can be first! 1 Corinthians 4: 9 says,

"For I think that God has displayed us, the apostles, last, as men condemned to death; for we have been made a spectacle to the world, both to angels and to men." (Read also 1 Corinthians 9)

Prophetic Utterances and Rebellion

Many times, people receive a prophetic word that brings them into rebellion because it was not coming from God and the giver has a motive. It is critical to test the character, to test the Fruit of the Spirit, ensuring that the person is:

1. Walking in integrity,

2. Submitted to a pastor

3. An active member of a local church.

4. Living a submissive lifestyle,

5. Not a loose cannon walking from church to church,

6. Not walking in the spirit of Jezebel or Absalom.

Know that any word given to you instructing you to rebel against your authority, or that carries with it any spirit of manipulation or control, you must never receive that word.

Prophets Must Embrace The Will Of God

Paul the Apostle received the word from Agabus in Acts 21: 9 - 14. Paul took the word the seriously, but he didn't change his plan. He wanted the will of God to be done.

There are times we will receive a prophetic word, but we must carefully pray on how to proceed. Remember that according to 1 Corinthians 13: 9, all prophecies are given in part. Hence, we must seek God in prayer for the whole picture. For example, if you are given a prophecy that you will live in/move to Georgia, you must seek God yourself before moving to Georgia. Ask Him when you are to make that move and which city He wants you in; because while the Lord may have given you that word, He wants to give you greater details directly. Your moving to Georgia may not necessarily be immediate or as soon as it seems like a door is open. That move may take place five (5) years after that prophetic word was uttered. This, however, is a different situation from being sent.

You may be a leader within a Church and the need may be great in Georgia or any other state. God may impress upon the Apostle to send those who make themselves available to go to that location. As they obey, there are serious blessings they will receive, because they are under authority and have followed the instructions of their leader.

I have had many leaders under my charge who have followed the instructions the Lord gave me to give them; and they have received tremendous, long-term blessings as a result, including marriage, children, and new business.

So, we must always pray for the Lord to show us the whole picture or we do as Mary did in Luke 2: 19 – 20 and ponder on it. When she received the prophetic word from Gabriel, the Scripture says she pondered. Many people after receiving a prophetic word, because they failed to seek God for the full picture, they proceed to walk away from:

1. Their mentor,

2. The state/parish/town/region in which they currently live,

3. Their job

To enter fulltime ministry and after making the decision, they lose all. Then, many of them become bitter, angry with God and turn away from Him and reject the prophetic word and ministry. Recognize that even where God gives a word that someone will die, prayer can change things and gives additional years. The prophetic is needed in this time and prophecy needed for this hour.

A Prophet of God is a spokesman, one who speaks the word of God. He/She must carry a divine message. The Prophet's message is God's message, not their own and their message must line up with the Word of God. They must help to build the local churches; they must always speak for the poor and the voiceless. Jesus was also a Prophet, as was Silas in Acts 15: 32, and Agabus 21: 8 – 14.

In addition to this, there are many who believe women should be silent, but there were four (4) virgin daughters in Acts 21: 9, who prophesied. There was also Huldah, in 2 Chronicles 34: 22 and Anna in Luke 2: 36 – 38. Who said women cannot prophesy? These scripture shows otherwise.

All can prophesy, but not all are prophets. A prophet functions in that office 24 hours per day. 1 Thessalonians 5: 20 – 21 tells us we must never despise Prophecy. Hold on to what is good when given a prophecy, test the word.

According to 1 Corinthians 12: 29, 1 Corinthians 14: 1, 5 and 39, 1 Corinthians 14: 13, all can prophesy.

Chapter 8

WISDOM AND PROTOCOL FOR LOCAL PASTORS

As God continues to reform the Body of Christ, it is critical for local churches and leaders to set up rules and protocol that will govern their churches. Many local churches are going through problems because they have not set a standard for their household (church/ministry). The following are keys of wisdom for Pastors and Leaders:

1. **Never** go into another Pastor's church and recruit people from their church to build up whatever you are planning. Furthermore, do not give out prophetic words to those members and collect seed/offering from them to do so; you are in fact stealing from another man's house!

2. Local Church Pastors **must** ensure that when visiting Pastors are allowed in, any private prophetic word given by them to their members must be done in the presence of one of your Pastors or Ministers.

3. **Always** use one of your strongest Ministers whom you can trust to carry out Armor Bearer functions for or to give assistance to the visiting Pastor. By doing so, you might avoid church splits and problems ahead.

4. **Recognize** that many Pastors who go to other Pastors' churches to preach, they moment they walk in, they are hit with envy and jealousy at what they see. As a result, they begin to find faults, ways and means to undermine the host Pastor(s) and engage in issuing their personal contact information to the members, befriend them and then pull them out! When a Preacher comes into your 'house', he/she is also subject to your authority and the rules of the house. Most local Pastors **do not** have rules, hence what they have built and labored for in the ministry can be torn down in a day.

5. One of the roles of a Shepherd is to ensure that you **protect** the flock. Hence, there are certain parts of the household that must be off limits to any visiting Minister.

6. Not everyone that comes in is about souls or is interested in edifying the Body. Most often they are about power, money and boosting their religious resume. It is very important for you as the local Pastor to teach your flock about the difference between the Gifts and the Anointing.

7. Understand and accept the fact that visiting Pastors does not grow a ministry. Prayer, Fasting, Evangelizing and Empowering do, through the power of the Holy Spirit. Many who come in do not care one iota about your hard work to build the ministry. You as the Local Pastor have the right to eat the fruit of your labor. Many Pastors labor, but those with whom they have labored oftentimes neglect to be a blessing to their local Pastor(s). The visiting Pastor is not the one who should be honored more than the Host/Local Pastor

8. Never invite a Pastor to minister to your church, or for spiritual covering because they are popular/famous. The kingdom is not about popularity and fame; it is about the Holy Spirit. Many seek for covering trying to get connected to big names, but through experience over the years, the majority of such Preachers and Leaders are only interested in their own ministry, not in yours. So while they have received favor, they do not extend such favor to others. When you encounter problems, you can hardly reach them for help. Many of them believe and teach that they do not

sow down, they sow up! Recognize that the Law of Seedtime and Harvest lets us know that every seed sown has to go down (into the earth) before it can come up! The fact that Jesus came and laid His life down for us, He sowed down and became poor for us to be rich! Think about this, when you literally look up what do you see above you? The sky! You will never see soil above your head it is always below your feet! Soil is required for sowing, so the principles of life itself is that something must go down for something to come up!

9. Network with Pastors who are willing to pay their own fares to come and fellowship with you and pour into you. It does not mean that you are not to take care of them and sow to them too; but those are often the ones with genuine motives.

10. Do not seek spiritual covering only for the purposes of access and impartation to you! You can contribute in return even prayer and other kinds of support! Look for covering from those who will live holy. It's not about the 20% (or however much it may be) that you would give to the Covering Ministry. Covering is a dual relationship – support goes both ways.

11. **Always** seek the Lord when establishing fellowship, relationship and networking. There are different levels. Remember, there are many out there in the fields with titles and titles can be bought. Many out there have split churches and

were operating rebelliously and without being under any authority. Don't watch the gift, *watch the Fruit!*

Chapter 9

ORDER IN THE CHURCH: SEXUAL PURITY

The cry locally and globally regarding sexual impurity in the Church on the part of the church leader leaves a lot of questions and opportunities. Were those with the titles of Bishop or Pastor within the local church afraid to address these serious matters because they were afraid of financial fallout and popularity? Everyone needs to really read and seek to understand 1 Corinthians 5. We need to judge within the church and let God deal with the world.

The Church seriously needs to look at how they select leaders. Are they selected by level of education or societal status? Leaders must be selected by the Holy Spirit and the Word, particularly Acts 6; 1 Timothy 3: 6, Luke 6: 12 – 17.

Is the Church putting young converts and people who are consumed with pride in positions of Leadership in the Church? Those who are untested (1 Timothy 3: 6)? These days, people turn into Bishops and Apostles overnight and have quite a large following thereafter without them being tested or proven.

When a leader of a church – whether Pastor, Bishop or Prophet – commits sexual sins openly, and it is exposed, they are still kept in the position without correction or restoration and then they call it grace! (Galatians 6: 1) Part of the restoration process includes discipline; for example, putting them to sit down for a year while they receive counselling.

If the church supports common-law relationships or marry those who are unequally yoked according to the Scriptures (2 Corinthians 6), then it means the church is also upholding sexual impurity and opens the door for such.

What do we say about Worship Teams and Musicians? They are now operating like stars and many of them are walking in sexual impurity, when they are supposed to be the most holy ministry in the church. Yet we allow them to operate and that opens the door to sexual immorality and defilement of the congregations. (*Read IN HIS PRESENCE by Pastor Michelle Lyston*) They mix with the world and think God is okay with it. Because we no longer allow the Holy Spirit, the Word of God and Jesus Christ to be the Center, the Body of Christ is now paying the price. If one belief is not lining up with the Word of God, then we are not even supposed to listen to them (read Galatians 1: 8).

Many attend churches, but did God lead them to where they are going or is it simply a physical attraction?

Many are turning away from the Church because of the sexual impurity they see in the church. Sadly, there are leaders in the church carrying on the same things that are done in the world – sexting, pornography, X-rated movie-binging and call themselves men of God, mighty prophets, mighty apostles – to say the least, their lifestyles leave much to be desired.

If people are "burning", God desires that they get married. God requires a holy lifestyle. The Pastors must take a stand to protect the young converts when they come to the house of the Lord. They cannot be coming in from the abuse and immorality, only to come right into much of the same in the place that should be a safe haven and sanctuary for them to be healed and made whole for God.

We also need to take a stand with the dressing. The attire of many today in the house of the Lord is atrocious. Prophets preaching in tight pants, tight jackets and/or underwear in plain sight. Some come with their shirts partially unbuttoned to advertise themselves. None of that reflects Jesus.

Sadly, there are women of God, both married and unmarried, who preach in clothing that are extremely tight and/or short, showing cleavage, and/or too thin, so that too much of what is private becomes publicly visible. For some of those who are married, their husbands cannot correct them on that issue because they (the women) let them know categorically, that they can wear what they want when they want.

All must remember that they are not to make themselves stumbling blocks for others. Remember Psalm 1: 1, Romans 14: 13 – 23, and 1 Corinthians 8: 9 which says,

"But beware lest somehow this liberty of yours become a stumbling block to those who are weak."

Value Your Marriage – Don't Play!

A higher percentage of marriages are crumbling today, and some that look good on the outside are unstable within. Some are just for show to appease others and the children - and the issues that cause them to crumble are simple things like credit cards, bills, closet space, long working hours and the third-party influence (friends or family).

Never make decisions in your household based on the opinions of others. So what if your friends buy new homes, vehicles or get opportunities that you don't?

Advice is often taken from people whose marriages have failed, or who have never been married. There are even people who will starve their partners of time and sex by becoming occupied with other things, getting degree after degree, while their marriage is crumbling. They do it to compete. Remember, every marriage comes with a covenant and breaking these covenants carry serious consequences.

Always marry who God says for love and for fulfillment of purpose. Any other motives will bring pain and headaches. Remember that there are gold-diggers and opportunists out there on both sides. There are also very good actors around but when the costumes are removed, that is when you will see the true character. Then it will be too late for a refund.

Good men and women still exist but you must look beyond what the natural eyes see and trust God for His choice. Marriage is more than sex, more than the wedding ceremony. It is not a "Mills and Boon" situation - it is real life. There are no roses without thorns. When someone's marriage fails then everything else falls apart. That is the reason it is so valuable. Many times, when marriages fail, people become bitter, but they do not accept that they are not blameless.

Know this! Dating and having sex do not determine whether a person is marriage material or not, because there are actors who can play any role, and after the opening night, God help you!

How To Pray For Your Marriage

Prayer is the most important key when fighting for your marriage. The enemy wastes no time in launching attacks at us and at marriages, so we cannot waste any time either in countering the attacks.

Therefore, pray the following prayer points:

1. Uncommon unity – Pray that uncommon unity will exist between you both.

2. Discern the enemies of your marriage – Pray that you will both discern any Judases, Jezebels or Delilahs in your midst.

3. Soul Ties and Strongholds– Pray that God will break all soul-ties from past relationships; and all strongholds.

4. Evil Altars – That God will destroy every evil altar that has been established to bring down your marriage.

5. Marine Spirits/Marine Witchcraft – Pray that God will destroy every marine spirit working against your marriage and union. In order to know if marine spirits are working against your marriage (or if evil altars have been established), pay attention to your dreams. Where you see yourself having intercourse in your dreams or marrying

someone when you are already married, that is an indication of the presence of marine spirits attacking your union.

6. Sex life in the marriage and health – Pray that your sex life will be 'on fire'. Pray also for patience in each of you; as well as good communication between you both. Pray also for physical and emotional healing for each other.

7. Money and a Third party – Pray that neither money, nor a third-party will come between you. That includes relatives and friends.

8. Unity in prayer – Pray that there is unity in prayer and that the husband will wash his wife with the Word.

9. One Vision – Pray that you both will have one vision – one set of goals and directions – so that the family unit can go in one direction according to the Will of God.

10. Quality Time – Spend quality time with each other and ensure that neither withholds sex from each other.

11. Increasing Grace – Pray that God will increase grace, mercy, compassion and favor each day.

12. Singular View – Pray that God will give the husband eyes only for his wife and that the wife's breasts will satisfy her husband.

Chapter 10

FALSE GRACE WITHIN THE FIVEFOLD

Ephesians 4: 7 - 12

It is critical for us to understand that to every gift in the Fivefold Ministry, Jesus Himself has assigned a specific grace. Verse 7 of the scripture says,

"But to each one of us grace was given according to the measure of Christ's gift."

When a person takes on a Fivefold office that the Lord did not assign to them, then they are functioning under a false grace which makes that person a counterfeit! It is sad that many people's lives have been ruined (both sinners and Christians) especially Christians who do not know the Word of God.

Purpose of The Fivefold Gifts

The number one purpose for which God gives gifts to people is to build them up and to edify the Church and equip the saints to build the Church so that they will not be moved by every wind of doctrine and act of trickery.

There are things that have been happening in the Body of Christ where doctrines have crept in which are not Scriptural and even titles that are not Biblical.

Time For Repentance

While we all in the Body of Christ need to look into ourselves first, those that God has truly given authority first need to ask questions such as, *"Did they issue authority to people who are not qualified in the office in exchange for monetary gain?" "Seeing that God is going to hold you accountable, what are you doing to deal with the damage out there that you have caused from that?" "Did you promote novices and people who were not tested in the faith, or have any spiritual genealogy in accordance with the books of Timothy and Titus that speak about Leadership?" "What is their spiritual genealogy?" "Whom do they serve?" "Who released them?" "Did the Holy Spirit validate them?"*

Serving In Leadership

Elisha served faithfully for 13 years before the double portion was released to him. Ezekiel was a priest before God allowed him to walk in the Prophetic. Jesus served 30 years for a 3-year ministry, and He still had to submit to John the Baptist, to be officially released into His ministry.

We know that there those who are false sheep (*the ones who believe they do not need to have a shepherd or submit to anyone*) and that they have created a market for lawlessness in the Body of Christ. It has also facilitated an environment where people do not know the false from the true. Jesus said that by their fruit you shall know them - not by their accuracy. None of these people have souls as a priority.

Leaders, when one in the Body of Christ suffers, ALL suffer. It is time to unite and begin to communicate – PRAY. If you cannot get recommendations on the faithful service of an individual or the individual cannot prove that they are doing work in ministry or have a congregation, then you need to think twice and revisit that application. We have seen people calling themselves Archbishop, Master Prophet and they do not even know how to function within a church/ministry in any capacity, not even to say that they have been a deacon or usher - and all of that puts souls at stake. People are dying under the deception.

According to the Ephesians 2: 20, if the Apostle and Prophet (according to the Fivefold Ministry) are the ones who bring Order, Interpretation of the Doctrine, Tactics and Strategies for the Building of the Church, and it is now compromised, then there are some serious showdowns ahead. Many who claim to be that, do not even know their job description from the Biblical standpoint.

Discernment, Doctrines and Deception

The Gift of Discernment of Spirits is critical to dealing with the deception that will be occurring in the End-Times. A person cannot discern accurately unless they know the Biblical Doctrine. The Bible states that in the last days, even the very elect will be deceived. While many focus on the gift of miracles, very few focus on doctrine – the most important thing. We must ask the question, *"Is the message being taught in line with the Word of God?"* *"Can the word you are hearing be confirmed with two or three Scriptures in the Bible?"*

We are seeing the New Age practices and principles taking over the Fivefold Ministry, of which the Prophetic Ministry is a part. The Holy Spirit is the **ONLY SOURCE** Who effectively brings true interpretation and opens our knowledge to allow us to understand the things of God, and the manifestation of the things of God. That is why we must ensure that the Holy Spirit is the first and foremost in our church as there are many other spirits operating through man bringing the Spirit of Error in the midst.

Doctrine is a set of beliefs or teachings relating to a particular subject, dogma, precept or teachings. Doctrine can either make, break or kill you. When Satan went to Eve in the Garden of Eden, he started to teach her a doctrine of lies and error, that pulled her out of God's will. Satan knew they were in God's will and on the right track, so he began teaching her a doctrine first to pull her out of God's will. Most problems that exist in the Fivefold ministry, first begins with lying doctrines.

In Psalm 91 and Luke 5, the enemy tried the same doctrine of lies and error to pull Jesus out, but because Jesus knew the truth of the Word of God, He was able to speak that truth back to the devil and shut down his lies.

Satan always presents a doctrine that will give you quick results without suffering. He hates the cross. He wants us to focus on the crown without a cross, which is deception; but in order to get the crown, we must bear the cross.

Satan is about what the eyes can see. He rules by fear. God carries us through a walk of faith which leads to the supernatural. To walk into the supernatural, you must walk by faith. The devil wants us to walk through divination. Not because a person is prospering does it mean that God is with him. Prosperity is not an indication that we are in right standing with God. There are many within the Fivefold who are living lavishly, but are serving the devil. Never forget Matthew 7: 21 – 23 which says,

"Not everyone who says to Me, 'Lord, Lord,' shall enter the kingdom of heaven, but he who does the will of My Father in heaven. Many will say to Me in that day, 'Lord, Lord, have we not prophesied in Your name, cast out demons in Your name, and done many wonders in Your name?' And then I will declare to them, 'I never knew you; depart from Me, you who practice lawlessness!'

So, the question is, if a person says *"Lord, Lord"* but does not do the Will of God, can there truly be Lordship without their obedience to Jesus Christ? Recognize, that Self-Deception is a mere verbal profession of Lordship without obedience to the Will of God. It is even possible for a self-deceived person to exercise a spectacular ministry using the authority of the Scripture, and in the name of Jesus, without walking in the genuine obedience to God and His Holy Spirit.

Everything we do, according to Matthew 7: 24 – 27 and 1 Corinthians 3, must be built on the solid Rock. Every Fivefold Ministry will be tested in the End-Time to see whether or not it is of God. The Holy Spirit will test it by fire to prove its substance.

There are many doctrines out there that have crept in the Church – doctrines of the Pharisees and Sadducees, doctrines that promote Self, doctrines without any theological truths, and doctrines promoting the lie that there are no more Apostles, Prophets or Spiritual Gifts.

Furthermore, they continually ignore Ephesians 4: 11, 1 Corinthians 12 and 1 Corinthians 14. In addition to this they tell people not to speak in tongues and go as far as calling it gibberish. This is why we have weak churches with so many of the leaders being a part of the occult. If there are no Apostles and Prophets – where they are each mentioned 83 times and 172 times respectively – then there are no more Pastors – mentioned only once in the Bible. This is what we call the spirit of the Anti-Christ operating within the Church.

Any teaching or doctrine that diminishes the power and presence of God within our lives and the local church, it is a teaching or doctrine of the devil. 2 Peter 2: 12 calls those who teach these doctrines "brute beasts". Paul speaks in 1 Timothy 6: 3 – 6, of the importance of Sound Doctrine. Paul revealed that the necessity of sound doctrine that all teaching is to be judged with the Word of God because some teachers are inflated by their own importance. Some add and substitute constant hair-splitting doctrines for the wholesome teachings of Jesus Christ. People also create doctrines for monetary gains and control. Why do you believe most Pastors are afraid of the gifts of the Holy Spirit manifesting in their church? Because they are afraid that things about their lifestyles would be revealed to those within the congregation, so they suppress those gifts, fight them out of the church, in order to maintain control. They know the people will not seek God for themselves as they have been getting away with it all these years. This is why the Fivefold Ministry is to equip the Church – the people – for the work of the ministry. But, how are we going to fully function and be the effective servants of the Lord if we are not grounded with the truth? The enemy has succeeded in keeping many blind. However, God is raising up Fivefold Teachers and Prophets to rebuild, prepare and edify the Body of Christ.

Chapter 11

KNOW THE SCOPE OF YOUR CALLING

Many times, in the business arena and in the Church, leadership will get frustrated, and companies and churches struggle at times because they are unable to service those within. Until you identify who you are called to and where your greatest support lies, who supports your business/church, you will not move forward.

Luke 4: 18 - 19, says,

"The Spirit of the Lord is upon Me, because He has anointed Me to preach the gospel to the poor; He has sent Me to heal the brokenhearted, to proclaim liberty to the captives and recovery of sight to the blind, To set at liberty those who are oppressed; To proclaim the acceptable year of the Lord."

My calling is to the poor in spirit, poor in finance, to set the captives free and to bring healing to the brokenhearted and recovery of sight to those who are blind spiritually and physically.

So if you are a prostitute, if you messed up, if you are a misfit, if you are rejected, or if you are a sinner or you are unrighteous - WELCOME! I am not called to righteous people, nor religious people, nor to those who have already arrived.

Paul was called to the Gentiles so God gave him the grace to deal with the Gentiles. He was set apart (Romans 1: 1 - 7) Many leaders - whether business or church - are spending too much time focusing on the wrong areas. Some even get disheartened and discouraged when certain people within the society do not accept them. You will not be accepted by everyone in the society - it is not Scriptural.

The Pharisees did not accept Jesus, and neither did His own city/town. When God gives you an assignment, keep going, keep doing good! Give hope to people! Stop moping and groping and focusing on those who criticize you and reject you.

Do an analysis and see who your biggest supporters are and focus on them; those who genuinely help you.

1) Who are your biggest clients?

2) Who always supports your work no matter what?

Those who are called to you will follow and support you. Recognize that you are not called to everybody.

Organizations fall when they change their mandate. Many companies are going into markets and territories that pull them away from what makes them great. Recognize that while businesses must be willing to take risks, they also need to draw the line between taking risks and shifting from the vision. What if KFC decided to open a supermarket chain; or if Digicel phone company or AT&T started selling Life Insurance?

Acknowledge and embrace your difference and run with it. Many churches are diverting from the mandate - even transforming to attract a certain set of people; or doing things which are not Scriptural. Now the many churches are becoming a laughing stock. Jesus did not try to fit in at all. Stick to your mandate despite the challenges. Know your clientele, know your sheep. Many times, the poor are more appreciative of the work you do and the sacrifices made and they need your difference.

Embrace Your Difference

Many Pastors today say they are called to the rich, but the rich do not truly need God until they become poor. Some of these church leaders today want to emulate Dr. Phil or Steve Harvey or John Maxwell – they simply need to be themselves. Many politicians are trying to be like President Barack Obama. One thing about President Trump – whether he was loved or hated, he never tried to be like anybody else, he was himself – take it or leave it. Quite a few Women of God try to be like or sound like Prophetess Juanita Bynum, but all they need to be is themselves.

Do not try to change your personality. Only those who embrace their difference (that is, accept what makes them different), and embrace the scope of persons to whom God has called them, will succeed in identifying and accomplishing their God-given task. David was a misfit. Several tried to change him even his mode of dress to keep him within tradition, but he did not fit in it. If he did not take off the traditional and just be himself, he would not have survived Goliath. Always remember this, *your difference is there to deal with what is to come, not for what already exists.*

Have you ever heard each time something goes wrong that the only solution that can come is to pass a law to make something work? The only solution we can find to any issue is to *'pass a law'*. Passing a law may not be the best solution at all times. It may even bring greater oppression. Interestingly, while they are passing these laws, they are not passing laws to hold themselves accountable.

Chapter 12

CALLED TO MINISTRY

Are you called to Ministry? If you are called to ministry, it is never an overnight thing. In the same way that those in other professions – doctors, pilots, lawyers – must go through a period of preparation, Ministry preparation requires even greater. The Holy Spirit is the One Who carries us through the preparation.

If we look at all the great men in the Bible – Joseph, Elisha, David, Moses, Peter and our Savior Jesus Christ – they went through a preparation before and even after they were called. Moses had to tend his father-in-law's flock. David had to tend his father's sheep. Elisha was a supervisor on his father's farm. Peter was a fisherman, and Jesus was trained by His step-father. They all have one thing in common – they were faithful and loyal, even before they were called to ministry.

We go through a process of being Called, Chosen, Commissioned and Sent. Each person must go through a process before they are Commissioned and then Sent. Now if you are interested in Ministry, you must do your own research to see how many years of preparation each person went through. God ordinarily takes us through several tests – the Time Test, the Word Test, the Patience Test, the Wilderness Test, Servanthood and Submission Test, the Honor Test, the Heart Test, the Test of Being Misunderstood and Discouraged, and several other tests, all designed to bring forth the Fruit of the Spirit within us.

1 Corinthians 14: 33 reminds us,

"For God is not the author of confusion but of peace, as in all the churches of the saints."

Many times, people will get a prophetic word – not from their leaders, but from someone on the outside of their church/ministry – to start a church/ministry of their own. They do not recognize that if it is the Lord Who is actually saying this, then He would also give the proper timing and the specific instructions as well as ensure that He has qualified the person in terms of their service, level of honor, submission, loyalty and their knowledge and understanding of His Word.

Oftentimes, people release themselves from their service and place to which they are called; but let it be clear that a person cannot release themselves, nor can they promote themselves, nor can they appoint themselves. There are many in ministry who are without a mantle. A mantle is symbolic of authority, leadership, responsibility and was the official garment of prophets, and it signifies sacrifice, commitment, the gifts and the call of God as well as the purpose to which they are called. Similarly, a person with a rod and a staff would represent responsibility and authority. The prophet is covered with God's authority, and keeps you from the elements. A mantle is something that is given by the Holy Spirit and can also be passed on. Jesus Himself had to be validated by the Holy Spirit in the form of a dove. (Matthew 3: 16 – 17). Many believe buying a Tallit and walking around with it is a mantle or gives them a mantle. (See 1 Kings 19: 13; 1 Kings 9: 13; 2 Kings 8: 13 – 14; Zechariah 13: 4; 1 Samuel 15: 27)

God wants each person in the Body of Christ to bear fruit; but that cannot happen unless you are planted (Psalm 92). Many who released themselves into ministry on their own, when they fail, they blame others for their failure. They say people are praying against them. The truth is that God did not validate them in the first place, hence they did not have a mantle to deal with the enemies nor the elements that came against them. We should never forget the sons of the prophets and what was asked of them when the axe head fell.

Types of People God Uses

It is critical that each person within the Fivefold Ministry to be utilized to do the work of the ministry. No one should be idle. Many times, you hear people who would asked the question: *"What is my calling?" "Can God use me?"* (Luke 1: 26 – 55).

God uses those who desire to do His will. Mary did not give an excuse to do God's will, because she wanted to do God's will. She did not complain about her work schedule, she did not put her personal vision before God's will. God uses people who **desire** to be use and those who are listening to Him. He uses those who are willing to pay the price (Luke 1: 38.), those willing to sacrifice, those who are willing to walk away from their comfort, friends and family. Those who are willing to step out by faith, those who are willing to listen to the critics while doing God's work. Those who are willing to trust His promise. (Genesis 12.)

God uses simple, ordinary people; those who love the supernatural, those who love Him and believe in Him. God uses imperfect people. For example:

1. Abraham – was an old man with a lot of family problems

2. Noah – was a drunk

3. Jacob – was a con-man

4. Leah – was very ugly

5. Joseph – was a prisoner

6. Moses – was a murderer with a speech impediment

7. Gideon – was a thief and coward

8. Samson – was a womanizer

9. Rahab – was a prostitute

10. David – was an adulterer

11. Timothy and Jeremiah – were youth

12. Naomi – was a widow and she was bankrupt

13. Judas – was a thief.

So, God does not call the equipped, He **equips** the Called. It is not about your ability; it is about your availability. God uses common people. (Judges 6: 14 – 16; 1 Corinthians 1: 26 – 27.) God turns ordinary people to extraordinary people. He removes the idols from our lives, purges and cleanse us. He uses those who are bold and courageous, he does not use cowards because cowards are driven by fear and so, are unstable and will betray you at the drop of a hat.

God can place a calling on your life, but cannot use you because you have forfeited that call, or you have not completed the process He put you through to use you for His Glory. For this reason and more, Matthew 20: 16 says, "For many are called, but few are chosen."

God called 32000 with Gideon, but only 300 were selected. He uses those who are confident in Him and live a holy lifestyle. When God calls people and they refuse to be used, it may result in calamity that will come up on them. (Proverbs 1: 24 – 26.) He calls the poor and make them rich. (James 2: 5.) God does not call the eloquent.

Jesus called the untrained, the uneducated, simple, and child-like. He called the weak, He called the despised, the poor, the foolish. (1 Corinthians 1: 26 – 31.) He called those, to make those who considered themselves as wise of this world to look foolish. (1 Corinthians 1: 20 – 28, 18-22.)

Each time He calls us, He equips us with spiritual gift(s). The Holy Spirit is the Giver of Spiritual Gifts. The gifts that do not belong to us, and are to be used for the Kingdom of God. We should never compete with the gift(s), but rather be used to complement each other. We must use our gift(s) to change the world, to solve problems, to help people as God's representative(s) on earth. Never sit down on the gift(s) - use it to touch someone's life. If God gives you the gift of Healing, use it to bring healing. If He gives you the gift of Miracle, use it to change lives. Give with a willing heart. If each person within the Body of Christ was utilizing the gift(s) that they were given by God, then there will be less crime and violence, less poverty, better political representative(s). When we fail to use the gift(s), God will remove it/them.

Pray this prayer:

"Father in the name of Jesus, I come to You right now, I repent of being selfish. Open my eyes and reveal to me, the purpose of the gift(s) and talent(s) that You are giving me, in Jesus' name. Amen"

Chapter 13

THE WATCHMAN

The Word of God tells us about the Watchman in Isaiah 21: 6 – 10, Isaiah 26: 10 – 12, Ezekiel 33: 7, and Amos 3: 7. The term "watchman" is generally defined as "one who keeps watch – one who looks out, a custodian, a century, or a scout." God Himself is a Watchman – He watches over us all and He never slumbers nor sleeps.

A Watchman is always looking out for illegal activities, positive or negative things that are approaching — whether the city, church or nation. The watchman also protects moral values within a nation. They are watching property, they watch for threats coming against organization, movements and activities. For example: A police officer is a watchman; homeland security officers are watchmen in the physical realm.

Within the Church, there are Christian watchmen who are assigned to watch both spiritual and natural activities that take place within a nation and globally. A Watchman must be always at his post to sound the alarm when danger is approaching a nation, an organization. Nothing should come up within any organization by surprise if a watchman is fully functioning in that organization. A Watchman must always sound the alarm for any approaching danger.

The Watchman is accountable to God and the Leaders that they serve within the organization. God speaks to watchmen through dreams and visions, through the word of God, through prayer or through the Rim of the Spirit which is the invisible rim, and through observation. The position of a Watchman is a serious one. There is evidence in the Bible in the book Nehemiah where even watchmen watch watchmen. Watchmen should watch and report of common dangers approaching Family, Church or Nation etc.

They are many watchmen throughout the world today. There are local watchmen such as our Police Department/Force and Security Guards, and international watchmen such as the **INTERPOL** *(United Nations: International Criminal Police Organization)*, **the FBI** *(United States of America: Federal Bureau of Investigation)*, **The KGB** *(Russian: Komitet Gosudarstvennoy Bezopasnosti - translation Committee for State Security)*, **The New Scotland Yard** (London), and **the Mossad** *(Israel: short for*

HaMossad leModi'in uleTafkidim Meyuḥadim – Israel's National Intelligence Agency), and **the Church** worldwide.

Requirements of The Watchman

The symbol of the Watchman is a dog, and while one of the negative meanings of the dog symbol is "an enemy", the positive side of this symbol is the Watchman, and it denotes loyalty as well. If a dog begins to dig at every yard or eat from every yard, that dog will become blind, ineffective and can be poisoned. Other symbols of the Watchman include the eagle, binoculars and the shofar.

1. It is extremely important that watchmen of both the natural/physical and the spiritual realms avoid compromise, gossip, and familiarity at all costs; their motives must always be right as God will oftentimes show the watchmen pending danger in dreams and visions, and it is important for watchmen to be spiritually ready to receive the information from the Lord.

2. Watchmen must know the meanings of Signs and Symbols and must understand the meanings of Colors and Numbers. They must also be skilled in the Word of God – always praying, and must always give accurate reports according to Matthew 13: 16 – 17.

3. Watchmen must be able to see what others cannot see. They must have the ability to hear what others

cannot hear. They must have the ability to discern the enemy, they must always know God's will and His ways, and, they must:

i. See (with their spiritual eyes)
ii. Hear (with their spiritual ears)
iii. Understand (discern)

No watchman must be spiritually blind, dumb, deaf or without discernment. This would disqualify them from being a watchman according to Matthew 13: 14 – 15. The Watchman must see the plan of the enemy and blow the trumpet – warn of danger. They must be alert, because they are the security of the city, the Church. They must be watching while the city is sleeping to safeguard those within. They cannot be lazy and/or sleeping at the post because, people's lives are at stake. They must see what is ahead and cancel it out with intercession, or, report it to their superiors/leaders, so that the necessary actions are taken, because under your watch, within your hands, there is life and death, blessings, breakthrough, protection, deliverance, impending danger, fasting and prayer. So, each time the Watchman blows the trumpet, each person should take the warning seriously. (Isaiah 21: 11 – 12. Joel 2: 28 – 29.)

We are now seeing many nations that are suffering, experiencing famine and disaster or another danger overtaking those nations because the watchmen are sleeping. We also see families breaking up, children perishing, church splitting, and church leaders falling, because the watchmen are sleeping. (Ezekiel 33:1 – 9.) We must treat our watchmen better than how we treat our hairdressers, our designers, our chefs, our teachers or anyone else we believe do menial tasks, because they may decide what takes place tomorrow.

The Ministry of Watchmen is appointed by God; they must see and warn by blowing the trumpet. When they warn, if one refuses to take heed of the warning, the Watchman is not responsible for what happens to that person. But if the Watchman refuses to warn of the impending danger upon a city or an individual, the blood will be on his/her hands. Each person has the opportunity to accept or reject the warning of the Watchmen. God is raising up new Watchmen in the Body of Christ and within nations and He will be replacing those watchmen with blood on their hands. (Ezekiel 33: 7 – 8, Matthew 13: 37, Luke 9: 44 – 56.)

A Watchman should never be concerned or feel responsible when God gives a message. The job of a Watchman is to deliver the message to the people; the acceptance of the message has to do with the Holy Spirit. Even if they reject you and the message, you are free, there is no blood on your hands. As a Watchman, you should not be afraid of being called false or fake, we must warn sometimes our family members. Watchmen have the authority to cancel the plan of the enemy - anything that is not in God's will. For example: you are married, and you get a dream that you are married again, or about witchcraft, or any dream about immorality – as a

Watchman, you have the authority to bind, loose and cancel. (Jeremiah 6: 17, Habakkuk 2: 1, Ezekiel 3: 17, Number 14: 1 – 25, 2 Samuel 18: 24 – 25, 2 Samuel 13: 34, 2 Kings 9: 17, Songs of Solomon 3: 3 also talk about the Watchman.)

One of the main reasons why there is so much shooting within our schools, it is because the Watchman is no longer in position. We are seeing a lot of countries once vibrant with Christian principles, once vibrant with a lot of churches, but they are no longer. When we look at Europe and the United States of America, which were once vibrant, they are now dead and need to be revived. Watchmen must know the time of the night and the season in which they are watching. They should never be ambushed by the enemy. Their voices must be loud when delivering the message. (Isaiah 52: 8, Jeremiah 31: 6, Jeremiah 6: 17, Isaiah 21: 11 – 12.) The Watchmen must also work along with the Gatekeepers – the Security Guards at the gates, the Ushers within the Church, the Butler in the home, the Secretary/Administrative Assistant on the job – watchmen must work with all those who control the points of entry/access points, that is, the gate. (2 Samuel 18: 24 – 27.)

Chapter 14

APOSTASY AND SIGNS OF TIMES

2 Timothy 3: 1 – 9 says,

"But know this, that in the last days perilous times will come: For men will be lovers of themselves, lovers of money, boasters, proud, blasphemers, disobedient to parents, unthankful, unholy, unloving, unforgiving, slanderers, without self-control, brutal, despisers of good, traitors, headstrong, haughty, lovers of pleasure rather than lovers of God, having a form of godliness but denying its power. And from such people turn away! For of this sort are those who creep into households and make captives of gullible women loaded down with sins, led away by various lusts, always learning and never able to come to the knowledge of the truth. Now as Jannes and Jambres resisted Moses, so do these also resist the truth: men of corrupt minds, disapproved

concerning the faith; but they will progress no further, for their folly will be manifest to all, as theirs also was."

It is critical for everyone - whether believers or non-believers - to take note of this particular scripture. We need to focus on the different areas listed by Apostle Paul.

We are indeed in perilous times. Perilous means harsh, savage, difficult, dangerous, fierce, and grievous. As Children of God, we need to begin using the Word of God as a measuring point. When a leader or any Christian embraces an opinion contrary to the Word of God, they have already fallen into Apostasy and should be avoided. (2 Peter 2: 20 – 22). When a leader or any member of the Christian family begins to advocate for sin to become legal, you as a Christian need to avoid that person. Any Christian opinion or leader that is not in line with the Bible should be avoided. Everything a Christian says or does has to be in line with the Word. Once it is not in line, then that person has fallen from Grace. They are already in Apostasy and they need to go back to Calvary. It is very critical who we follow in this end time, because we are surely in the end time.

When a Christian leader who is a musician or singer starts to encourage people in New Age Movements, Transcendental Meditation, Yoga, Tattoos, Sexual Immorality, it is time for you to leave that church.

Prophets and their Messages

Galatians 1:8 says, *"But even if we, or an angel from heaven, preach any other gospel to you than what we have preached to you, let him be accursed."*

Any prophet's message that is promoting any ministerial office more than the office of Jesus Christ, do not follow them! If a prophet is preaching more about how accurate he is, rather than Jesus crucified, risen and ascended – which should be center of the message – do not follow them! No prophets should be exalting themselves above Jesus and the Holy Spirit. Even on flyers we see prophets having 3 or 4 pictures of themselves telling people to come and see them, but nothing is mentioned about Jesus or the Holy Spirit. Furthermore, true prophets draw the attention of the people to Jesus Christ - not to themselves. Every prophet must submit to the governing authorities within the local church. They have to be pastored, shepherded and taught. They are not under the old covenant anymore where they are accountable directly to God. There was no church in the Old Testament. Jesus restructured the Church according to Ephesians 4: 11, and 1 Corinthians 12: 27 – 28 which says,

"Now you are the body of Christ, and members individually. And God has appointed these in the church: first apostles, second prophets, third teachers, after that miracles, then gifts of healings, helps, administrations, varieties of tongues."

So they are set within the local church to establish and build the Church. There are many within the Body of

Christ teaching false doctrines. Some are even giving themselves names like "Forensic Prophets", "CSI", while others are teaching that accuracy makes one a true prophet – which is not true. Jesus said in Matthew 7: 15-20 which says,

"Beware of false prophets, who come to you in sheep's clothing, but inwardly they are ravenous wolves. You will know them by their fruits. Do men gather grapes from thornbushes or figs from thistles? Even so, every good tree bears good fruit, but a bad tree bears bad fruit. A good tree cannot bear bad fruit, nor can a bad tree bear good fruit. Every tree that does not bear good fruit is cut down and thrown into the fire. Therefore by their fruits you will know them."

Always look for the Fruit of the Spirit as in Galatians 5. Watch out to see whether or not they try to break up churches or pull people away. Always ask them, "*Who is your Apostle?*" If they say they submit to no one but God – **RED FLAG!**

Watch out for those who say they will release curses and/or send curses back to sender.

God is realigning His Church and putting things back in order, and only those who will line up, will be a part of the end time move. This realignment is also part of the structure being reinforced that the Church be fortified for the end time and move as an army.

Chapter 15

IDENTIFYING DECEPTION

Deception offers that which is desirable in the beginning but is destructive in the end! Satan came to Adam and Eve in the Garden and asked: *'Do you want to be like God?'* It was desirable in the beginning, but when both ate the Forbidden Fruit, they were driven from the Garden into the world.

God will allow deception that will drive many of us to read the Word of God, Pray and Fast! Deception comes to those who will walk by sight and not by FAITH! Many, in pursuit of quick riches or harbor greed or view things based on outward appearances are open to deception in this season. For example, if one trusts man more than God, one is open to deception.

Many judge based on eloquence, intellect, appearance and level of academic achievement to summarize people or make certain decisions; and if those are your criteria, you are also open to deception in this season. If we follow those criteria, we will always be deceived by politicians, 'Ponzi' type Schemers, False Prophets, False Teachers and more.

Deception comes when we are spiritually low. Many go for heights, few go for depth! Depth in God is greater than Height! When you have depth in God, you become rooted. From that standpoint, you reach greater heights when you are firmly rooted!

There are key Words and Scriptures to which we must pay great attention to in this time. Words such as Nimrod, Babylon, Spirit of the World, the Dragon. Scriptures such as the Book of Daniel, I John 2. Pay attention to your dreams and symbols such as snakes, cats, kisses, silver coins. The Holy Spirit is speaking as never before to His people, but many are not paying attention.

Do not be fooled by Social Network. There are different levels of Deception!

1. Self-Deception – I John 1: 8

2. Rebellion & Disobedience – Deuteronomy 28: 1 – 14; James 4: 17

3. Sexual

4. Spiritual

5. Moral & Ethical

6. Intellectual
7. Political

Recognize too that Lack of Patience and Pride will bring deception! The enemy will come as an angel of light!

It is sad to say, sinners are quicker to discern deception than Christians. We even see where sinners perceived more readily who Jesus was, while the religious ones could not! Matthew 24: 3 – 14 says:

"Now as He sat on the Mount of Olives, the disciples came to Him privately, saying, "Tell us, when will these things be? And what will be the sign of Your coming, and of the end of the age?" And Jesus answered and said to them: "Take heed that no one deceives you. For many will come in My name, saying, 'I am the Christ,' and will deceive many. And you will hear of wars and rumors of wars. See that you are not troubled; for all these things must come to pass, but the end is not yet. For nation will rise against nation, and kingdom against kingdom. And there will be famines, pestilences, and earthquakes in various places. All these are the beginning of sorrows. "Then they will deliver you up to tribulation and kill you, and you will be hated by all nations for My name's

sake. And then many will be offended, will betray one another, and will hate one another. Then many false prophets will rise up and deceive many. And because lawlessness will abound, the love of many will grow cold. But he who endures to the end shall be saved. And this gospel of the kingdom will be preached in all the world as a witness to all the nations, and then the end will come."

Many think that this Scripture refers to a local prophet in a church who makes an error and gives a word and is regarded as a False Prophet. But the Lord was speaking concerning the religious, social and political. There are many in Politics and in the Media who say they are Christians, but yet they do not ascribe to or believe in what the Word says – they have different views and ideologies. Take heed because not one of God's Words will fall to the ground!

If you are one who believes that a true prophet is one who gives you a word that comes to pass, you will be deceived. We are not under the Old Testament where prophets were judged solely on the accuracy of the prophetic word they uttered. Jesus said, if you want to know who a true prophet is, by their fruit you shall know them. (Matthew 7; Galatians 5) Remember, the devil is accurate too!

There are different principles we can use to judge prophecies/prophetic words. We are commanded to test the spirit. (I John 4: 1) whether they are of God, of self or of the devil. False prophecies lead to deception and manipulation. Every motive and hidden agenda must be tested. Why are most New Testament prophets of today are not effective? Most of them are politicians; and as such they cannot see beyond their favorite political party. Are the prophecies bringing edification, exhortation and comfort? It must agree with the Word of God; it must bear fruit and agree with the Holy Spirit. If a Word of Prophecy promotes disobedience against God's Scripture, it is not a true prophecy. (Deuteronomy 13: 1 – 3) Any prophecy given that is against Scriptural Guidelines is not of God. True prophecy promotes liberty and not bondage. Any prophecy that comes but does not give glory and honor to Jesus Christ is deception.

Test The Spirit (1 John 4: 1)

There are many things happening globally which have confused many and they wonder whether it is God or not. We have a responsibility to test the spirit behind every doctrine, teaching or manifestation of spiritual things – whether in the world or in the Church.

1. Anything that veils God's glory is not of God. Worship only belongs to God.

2. Anything that fails to honor Jesus Christ as first and foremost and the center of our faith, and the source of any spiritual manifestation is not of God.

3. Anything that presents Him as less than God is deception.

4. We cannot take Christ out of Christianity, nor can we remove the Cross, the Blood of Jesus, His Death and Resurrection from Christianity.

5. If you are operating in the Gifts of the spirit or any of the Ascension gifts and the glory is more centered on you than on Jesus and the Holy Spirit, then that is deception.

6. There is no such thing as Christian Yoga. That is not the Holy Spirit that is the Kundalini spirit.

Any message you hear, check to see if it is promoting Jesus Christ as Lord and Savior. If not, it is not God's Holy Spirit. Some of the functions of The Holy Spirit are:

i. He shows us things to come. (John 16:13)

ii. He washes, sanctifies, purifies and justifies. (Romans 15;16, 1 Corinthians 6:11; 2 Thessalonians 2:13; 1 Timothy 3:16; 1 Peter 1:2,22)

iii. The Holy Spirit produces fruit in our lives. (Galatians 5:22-23; Ephesians 5:9)

iv. He confesses Christ's Lordship. (1 Corinthians 12:3)

There are many spirits in the world – unclean spirits, spirit of man, spirit of error, anti-Christ spirit, Kundalini spirit and many more, but there is One Holy Spirit, and it is critical for us to test and know what spirit is in operation.

Beware of The Nicolaitans

The doctrine of the Nicolaitans is also the doctrine of Balaam – that good works bring salvation. Nicolaitan simply means "having power/victory (control) of the laity". (1 Peter 5: 1 – 3) Recognize, however, that feeding the poor and carrying out charity work is good, but that is not salvation – it is not what gets you to go to heaven.

Salvation means you are saved by grace through faith in Jesus Christ. In other words, you have accepted that Jesus is real, His life on earth and His sacrifice through His death on the Cross are real, His resurrection is real, and you accept Him as Lord of your life. Ephesians 2: 8 – 10 says:

"For by grace you have been saved through faith, and that not of yourselves; it is the gift of God, not of works, lest anyone should boast. For we are His workmanship, created in Christ Jesus for good works, which God prepared beforehand that we should walk in them."

The Nicolaitan doctrine focuses on wealth, title, power, honors and accolades as being the standard for being in right standing with God. It also says you can partake in sin because the law of God is no longer binding. So, it abuses and tramples on the Grace of God.

Recognize that while God wants us to have prosperity, it does not indicate that you are with God. In fact, 1 Timothy 6: 10 says,

"For the love of money is a root of all kinds of evil, for which some have strayed from the faith in their greediness, and pierced themselves through with many sorrows."

This doctrine has seeped into the Fivefold Ministry and has taken hold. Many Apostles and Prophets today, now want to be as the Episcopalians – wanting to dress and function as they do – thereby compromising their walk, the Gospel and the value of true salvation.

There are false teachers who have taken over the church and Jesus hated false teaching. Read every word for yourself in Revelation 2: 12 – 15.

Nicolaitans work closely with Jezebel, who teaches God's people spiritual adultery or fornication – meaning that while having a relationship with God, they are embracing false doctrines and performing actions opposite to God's Word and instructions.
Revelation 2: 5 – 6 says

"Remember therefore from where you have fallen; repent and do the first works, or else I will come to you quickly and remove your lampstand from its place—unless you repent. But this you have, that you hate the deeds of the Nicolaitans, which I also hate."

Nicolaitans are also paid prophets who utter curses and seduce God's people into sinning.

Beware of the falsehood of the Nicolaitan doctrine and recognize that true salvation is not by way of works, but by the Way Who is Jesus Christ.

Chapter 16

DEATH IN THE POT!
BEWARE OF FALSE DOCTRINES!

We are in a critical time now where false teachings are going to be more rampant now than ever before! False teachings have been plaguing the Church/Body of Christ! Never forget the Scripture in 2 Kings 4: 38 – 41

It is the responsibility of local Church Leaders to feed the people with the provision that God has given them. Many are not satisfied with the provision God has given for them so they are now going into other fields to gather herbs which are from wild vines – representing false doctrines – which bring death!

False doctrine brings death in the church. Any doctrine not built exclusively on the cross of Christ (1 Peter 1: 18 – 20) must not be tolerated. Only the undiluted Word of God can cure the Death which is in the pot! False

doctrine poisons and it poisons many when it is brought in and shared with the congregation.
Leaders should not take their eyes off 2 Timothy 4: 1 – 5.

These are the following things that leaders should look out for: Always use I Timothy 4 as a guide when preaching and teaching and when others are preaching and teaching.

When others are preaching and teaching – whether they are from within the Church or from the outside, always scrutinize the message and the doctrine. There is great Apostasy taking place! No minister should ever preach what they think is their view. It must always be the BIBLE VIEW!

Remember, False Doctrine defiles and destroys the flock. All doctrine must be established on Jesus and the Cross. He is the Center and the Owner of the Church! Nothing must take precedence over the fact that JESUS DIED FOR US TO RECEIVE SALVATION!

In I Timothy 4, the Holy Spirit speaks openly and prophetically that, in the latter times, many will depart from the faith and they will apostatize! They will deny the essential doctrine of Christianity.

The False Teacher is on the loose! False Teachers are teaching doctrines inspired by Satan and this will lead many astray including careless leaders who are not studying. (John 8: 44; Acts 2: 17; Hebrews 1: 2; I John 4: 1 – 6)

False Teachers are now on the rise! They are on the internet, social networks/media and they are very influential. Each time they release their venom, it spreads within the flock and contaminates the church. False Teachers will present 'Divine' inspiration in abandoning God's Word, they become de-sensitized to spiritual truth.

False Teachers attack Fivefold Ministries that establish order in the congregation. They call order manipulation and witchcraft!
False Teachers encourage and often support Dating and Fornication, Oral & Anal Sex and Masturbation.

Leaders from time to time need to do spot checks on the membership to see what doctrines are surfacing that they as leaders may not be aware of. Leaders also need to check what kind of study bibles are being used. Many are also reading books that are New Age based but they think it is spiritual!

A person who falls away from the true faith, falls prey to all kinds of traps that are alleged to make one more spiritual – such as False Asceticism.

Always keep your eyes on I Timothy 4 especially verses 4 – 5. Let no one deceive you about Food, Marriage or Sex. Many distracting conversations are emerging on issues such as Women in Ministry, Day of Worship, Marriage and Divorce, Submission and Prosperity.

All leaders must begin to expound on and apply the scriptures and also exercise the gifts that God has given them. Remember, the personal life of a minister must be as pure as their doctrine. A false prophet is not one who necessarily gives a word that does not come to pass; but Matthew 7 and Galatians 5 tell us that we must judge them by their lifestyle/their fruit. Are they touching God's glory? Are they brining people unto themselves more than Christ? Are they in open sin – sexually? Are they greedy? Do they have wrong motives? Do they believe in the Virgin birth of Jesus and His death and Resurrection?

All teachings must be judged by their agreement with the Word of God. (I Timothy 1: 3). Also, watch out for the Spirit of Error and Greed. (I Timothy 6: 3 – 6; I Timothy 4: 6)

A good teacher is constantly nourishing themselves with the Word. Once a minister's focus shifts from souls, then that person will begin to walk in error.

Please read the following Scriptures:

- ✓ Matthew 22: 29
- ✓ Galatians 1: 6 – 9
- ✓ 2 Timothy 4: 2 – 4
- ✓ 2 Timothy 3: 16
- ✓ 2 Peter 1: 21

Always remember that whatever man terms as inspiration must be consistent with the Bible. Not every inspiration is Biblical. There is a difference between inspiration and illumination! Illumination refers to the influence of the Holy Spirit which helps all Christians to grasp the things of God. We must seek to have Illumination. (I Corinthians 2: 4; Matthew 16: 17)

Misunderstood Scriptures and Words

Old Prophet, Young Prophet

Oftentimes there are Scriptures that are popular but often misunderstood. One such Scripture is I Kings 13 – Young Prophet, Old Prophet. Those who are immature or misinformed tend to quickly turn to this Scripture when they do not want to submit and are walking in disobedience. They often try to use this Scripture in the context of age citing that they are the young ones that the Lord is working with now and so they do not have to obey those before them including their shepherd. In no respect was this Scripture speaking about age or seniority.

In this Scripture – I Kings 13 – the Lord was speaking about the lifestyle of a prophet, and it meant that an 'old prophet' was one who was stuck in the old ways – and one who has fallen into apostasy; one who compromised the Word of God for material and other gain. It meant that an old prophet was one who had gone back to their old lifestyle and was no longer walking in truth. It also meant that they were no longer walking in the fruit of the spirit, but were instead walking in the flesh. Thus, that prophet backslid but still functioned in his/her authority like Balaam, and those who were on Jezebel's payroll.

The 'young prophet' referred to one who walked in truth, holiness and righteousness regardless of the cost. They had a holy lifestyle and did not tell people what they wanted to hear. Micaiah (I Kings 22) is one example of the Young Prophet and so is Jeremiah.

So, it is possible to be young in the faith and even young in age and still be an Old Prophet if your lifestyle does not line up with the Word of God. Whenever a person is not walking in the truth, God refers to that person as old; we must always remain Young! This is why as Christians, we cannot mix or fellowship with other Christians who are not walking in the truth or holiness. The Word even says we are not even supposed to eat (network or affiliate) with them. (1 Corinthians 5)

Favored, Called and Chosen

Many times, people will say they are walking in favor; but favor is something that one has to maintain with or through True Obedience (Deuteronomy 28: 1 – 14) Genuine Submission to Godly authority. (Luke 2: 49 – 52) Hence favor – like faith – has a measure. It increases as we continue to walk in God's perfect will. Favor also has to do with those to whom you submit and those you serve. For example, Ruth and Naomi, Elisha and Elijah, Jacob and Laban. Last year's favor cannot deal with this year's issues. When a person continually walks in disobedience, then that grace and favor will cease to exist.

Many times, people say that they are called and chosen by God, but remember that the Word says that many are called and few are chosen. To be chosen, a person must be able to pass the tests in the timing of God. Of the 32,000 that were called, less than 1% passed the tests; and these tests were simple instructions and required attention to detail and vigilance, as well as focus on the Kingdom. There must be a steadfast focus on the Kingdom!
While many say that they are called and chosen and cannot even submit to the leadership of a good mentor, they need to think again. Would the Lord give authority to the ones who will not / do not / refuse to submit to authority?

God's criteria for using someone within the Kingdom to carry out His will and purpose is higher and He will not change His Word to fit into our desire rather than His will.

Chapter 17

DESTROYING THE COUNSEL OF BALAAM!

Wisdom Outside The Box

Over the years there has been witness of people with great potential – personally and in ministry – get hit through the spirit of Balaam! The spirit of Balaam focuses on Money/Honor /Accolades! They prey on weak, confused Christians and on those who have a little influence. They are the ones who are behind most church splits; and when you have promising leaders or armor-bearers rising up they are the ones who give them lying prophetic words and pull them out of position.

Balaam took orders from Balak – a Moabite who was afraid of the growth and expansion of God's people.

For all Fivefold Ministry Leaders – Apostles, Prophets Evangelists, Preachers, Teachers and whoever is involved in Church Planting, the spirits of Balaam and Balak are always on the ready to attack. Some of them are over regions and call themselves "*Chief this*" and "*Master that*"! They are always quick to decree and prophesy curses. Anyone who does that – anyone who declares curses upon people is nothing but a warlock or witch!

The spirit of Balaam gives advice to disrupt your church and tells your people how to sin and how to walk in rebellion; they give wrong prophetic counsel. Balaam was not about souls, he was about material things.

Balaam boasted about his accuracy, however the jackass was more accurate than he was because the jackass could see the danger before him!

Have you ever seen a member who was quite alright this Sunday and then next Sunday he/she is a different person completely! Watch it!

I urge all those who are sending curses out against Christians and sinners or those giving 'wise' counsel to stop the growth and development of organizations or individuals to CEASE AND DESIST!!!!

Chapter 18

GOSPEL ARTISTS AND MUSICIANS ARE NOT NIGHTCLUB ENTERTAINERS

Music is considered a universal language. It has the capacity to transcend cultures, create moods, change the atmosphere, penetrate the human spirit, influence the heart and mind and soften the hard-heartedness of man. If properly administered, music can even help to reduce crime and violence, and heal the soul and body.

Gospel singers and musicians, as well as Psalmists must be called, anointed and appointed. Further to this, they must be held accountable, submitted to the authority of a Pastor within a local church. The Pastor must be their first leader – not their manager or booking agent. Gospel artistes of all kinds should be regulated, functioning in

Scriptural order (1 Chronicles 15: 16 – 22) because it is a holy capacity within which to function, and must not be treated as common.

I Peter 2: 9 says,

"But you are a chosen generation, a royal priesthood, a holy nation, His own special people, that you may proclaim the praises of Him Who called you out of darkness into His marvelous light;"

It simply means that such persons are not called to do what everybody else does in the way they do it; such persons are set apart, consecrated to God and must function to a higher standard, being part of the Royal Priesthood! Everything about them must be holy – their songs, how they put themselves together – even how they deal with people.
One cannot say that he/she is set apart, but looks like the world on the basis that he/she is trying to win the world!

Some female gospel artists are competing with Rihanna, Beyoncé and Lady Gaga with regard to their attire and how they carry themselves generally. For some male artistes, you do not know the difference between them and Usher, Justin Timberlake or Justin Bieber!

Our gospel artistes must recognize that *Preachers of LA* and *American Idol* are not the standard by which their ministries must be measured! Some pastors are compromising on keeping our gospel artistes accountable for their representation of the Kingdom and to the world. Most churches are now being transformed into nightclub settings with smoke effects and strobe lights.

Levitical Order

Gospel Singers and Musicians must recognize that they are considered (Scripturally) as part of the Levitical Order. So as the Levites did, they must fast, study the Word of God on a daily basis, and sometimes pull away from the public eye and go into the presence of God to receive fresh revelation from Him to bring transformation to nations, dealing with Spiritual Warfare, and even allow the wealth of the wicked to transfer to the just. (II Chronicles 20)

One of the major responsibilities of Gospel Artists and Musicians is to take us into God's Presence, not to entertain us. Another of their responsibilities is to set good examples for all those they reach. It is their responsibility to create an environment for solutions to come forth so that heads of governments, military personnel will receive solutions when facing a crisis. (II Kings 3: 14 - 27)

It is the singers and the musicians that should be influencing the tearing down of strongholds over a nation, so that justice, order and freedom can be maintained. (Psalms 149)

The condition within a nation is reflective of the condition of the praise and worship that is going up to God. Yes, politicians and others within the nation share the blame for the state of their nation. However, the state of the Praise and Worship that goes up to God, and the quality of ministry that comes from the Gospel Artists, Musicians has also played its role in the state of their nation.

It is the responsibility of the Church also to make every effort to pay their musicians and singers as David and Nehemiah did when they reformed the House of God, that we can keep them in order to maintain the Praise and Worship within the House of God – instead of being in every concert and show where the focus is not to glorify God, but to entertain and grow their fan base.

It is the responsibility of the Pastors of our Gospel Artists and Musicians to correct, rebuke, guide, nurture, teach, admonish and help them where they are going beyond the boundaries of Scriptural conduct, or are in rebellion and need to be brought back to basics and restored – among other things.

Finally, it is the responsibility of those who listen to and support our Gospel Artistes and Musicians, pray for them to continue to walk in the way of the Lord, and call them to a higher standard of ministering and encouraging the Presence of God on all present.

Chapter 19

JEZEBEL IN THE FIVEFOLD

Jezebel is one of the most common and most dangerous spirits that attack the Fivefold Ministry. This spirit causes church splits, chaos and confusion. One of the things that most Apostles and Pastors get fooled by, particularly when they are just starting out in ministry, is to focus on the gifts of an individual. The Bible tells us to focus on the fruit.

The Spirit of Jezebel may be intelligent, accurate, hardworking but they need healing and deliverance; and if they do not begin to submit within the local church, then they will call for "back-up" from the spirits of Manipulation, Control and Intimidation.

Most have been through hurt and abuse and refuse to forgive. Hence, as soon as they begin to get a platform, there will be chaos within your church.

Oftentimes, Pastors do not discern this spirit right away because they are close to them. They may be the number one prayer warrior within the church or the biggest tither, but it is a dangerous spirit and it has destroyed many Pastors and Fivefold Ministries. It is critical to identify those who possess the spirit of Jezebel and begin the course of deliverance if they are willing to do so.

Here are some things Jezebel does:

The Spirit of Jezebel:

1. Hates order within the local church.

2. Preys on weak leaders and also on those people who love to hear prophecies more than they do the Word of God.

3. Attacks the order and policies within the Church

4. Compliments you publicly while setting up plans to divide and conquer behind your back

5. Pulls people to themselves

6. Works from behind the scenes and carries out their acts

7. Puts others forward as a face while they carry out their activities

8. Works closely with the Spirit of Absalom

9. Is controlled by Leviathan

10. Is a good actor and an incessant liar; finds every reason not to repent, blaming others for his/her downfall.

The Spirit of Jezebel pretends as if he/she is filled with love and will even shed tears in order to attract compassion and pity, but that spirit is dangerous. The great prophet Elijah was afraid to face the Spirit of Jezebel and ran from it instead.

Recognize that Jezebel was of Royal lineage. While she became the wife of Ahab, the King of Israel at that time, she did not embrace Israel's God, but instead held on dearly to her idols. (1 Kings 16: 31 – 33).

The role of the Spirit of Jezebel is to kill the true prophets, bring people into an unholy lifestyle, to adhere to false doctrines, false religions and to gain control. Once she is not in control, she then releases her wrath. She also wants her own company of prophets to server her. She hates the Elijah and Elisha companies. Remember that there were eight hundred and fifty (850) prophets of Baal and Asherah who were loyal to her. She seeks to tear down the altar of God and move people away from prayer. She also steals the loyalty and removes the Head of the Ministry and the First Lady. She sees herself as more qualified than the First Lady.

She brings sin within the church, as well as false teachings, rebellion and is self-appointed. She leads the people into spiritual adultery or spiritual fornication – incites others to do evil. In Revelation 2: 19 – 23, the Lord says,

"I know your works, love, service, faith, and your patience; and as for your works, the last are more than the first. Nevertheless I have a few things against you, because you allow that woman Jezebel, who calls herself a prophetess, to teach and seduce My servants to commit sexual immorality and eat things sacrificed to idols. And I gave her time to repent of her sexual immorality, and she did not repent. Indeed I will cast her into a sickbed, and those who commit adultery with her into great tribulation, unless they repent of their deeds. I will kill her children with death, and all the churches shall know that I am He who searches the minds and hearts. And I will give to each one of you according to your works."

Be careful not to tell Jezebel your personal business and weaknesses, and certainly nothing about your marriage or any issues within it. This spirit will use that information and rip your marriage, business and personal life to shreds and then insert itself in as the solution.

The Spirit of Jezebel will compliment you and build up your confidence or ego. For example, that spirit may say, *"You are the most anointed person and you deserve better"* and such things. If you are an associate pastor or prophet, they will tell you to go and start your own ministry. As a result, they will move you out of position and cause you to be destroyed.

The Spirit of Jezebel goes in the midst of a husband and wife ministry team and try to convince one that he/she is more anointed than the other, and will say they like to hear that one more than the other.

In 1 Kings 21, we see how dangerous the Spirit of Jezebel can be. It plotted against and ultimately murdered Naboth for his vineyard. Read this Scripture carefully and you will see how skilled this spirit can become. Jezebel went as far as stealing the Royal Seal – which is fraud – and asked the nobles to proclaim a fast, bestow honor upon Naboth and then get false witnesses against him. Ensure that when prayer and fasting is called for within the Fivefold church, you are fully aware of the motives of the fasting and prayer and ensure that it is not Jezebel who is in charge of that Prayer and Fasting. That spirit may be calling for prayer and fasting to unseat the Pastor and First Lady without their knowledge, and pull innocent people in – opening the door for attacks on them and on the ministry.

The Spirit of Jezebel is very seductive – a silver-tonged fox, and is very skilled with the power of suggestion. It plays leader against leader and always questions the Lord's Word. Furthermore, they have no respect for authority. Interestingly, they think they can fix what the leader cannot fix and when the leader makes a decision, they rebel against them. They link with like personalities.

The spirit of Jezebel also, in Revelation 2: 20 - 23, calls herself a prophetess. They bring false teachings within the church – such as Yoga, and call it "Christian Yoga"; Transcendental Meditation or TM, as well as the Kundalini spirit – a counterfeit of the Holy Spirit. So, this spirit will introduce Canaanite religions into the church according to 1 Kings 11: 29 – 31; 2 Kings 9: 22, 2 Kings 18: 4 & 9; and Romans 6: 1 – 23.

Wherever there is famine within a nation or a lack of Spiritual revival, you can trace it back to the spirit of Jezebel.
For the Church to effectively fight Spiritual warfare, they have to conquer the spirit of Jezebel.

Dealing With Jezebel

Not every prophet has been given the grace to deal with Jezebel. God had to train Elisha and raise up Jehu in order to deal with her. Elisha represented the Spiritual aspect and Jehu represented Civil authority. This spirit is not confined to the church, it operates in Church, Civil Governments, Families, Media – all facets of life. No weak leader, nor anyone intent on being "politically correct" can defeat the spirit of Jezebel.

1. In order to begin to deal with the spirit of Jezebel, Elijah had to rebuild the altar of God. So, it means a leader must have a strong prayer life. Prayer is key to dealing with Jezebel.

2. Every leader dealing with Jezebel must close the door to sexual immorality.

3. If a leader has a weakness, they must submit that weakness to God, come before Him in repentance and desist from engaging in those weaknesses any further. That leader has to walk in holiness, with God, so they can stand against the plots of Jezebel.

4. Build God's government on the Word of the Lord and the Name of the Lord.

5. Always establish prayer within the schools, businesses, and all organizations.

Never deal with the spirit of Jezebel based on emotions – including anger or pity – that pulls you right into her trap. Be careful what you take from that spirit, because they will be generous initially, but they will come for payback later on; and as soon as you disagree with them on any matter, then you will see the flip side of that generosity.

Never underestimate the spirit of Jezebel. Elijah, had to run away leaving his servant behind in order to escape Jezebel. He ended up under a juniper tree – which means he ended up in isolation away from the will of God wondering if he was called or not. (1 Kings 19: 1 – 10)

Never seek any other god for information, seek only the Almighty God for the direction you need to receive for His creation.

Chapter 20

GOD STILL SPEAKS

Many within the society – both in the Church and the Secular community – are always attempting to mock the fact the God still speaks. They see those who say they have received a message or a Word from God as being insane or fanatical. The reason the globe is suffering the way it is today is as a result of the fact that man refuses to listen to God on a daily basis. (Deuteronomy 28: 1 – 14)

Interestingly, many seek alternative ways of hearing about what is to come through psychics, mediums and such. Others pay millions per hour to get a word from the devil, only to defile themselves and put their souls in jeopardy with God.

What if both secular and church leaders were listening to the voice of the Lord? We would be much further advanced globally.

How Does God Speak?

God speaks to us through:

1. **The Holy Spirit** (John 14: 26)

2. **Dreams and Visions** (Acts 2: 17; Joel 2: 28; Job 33: 14 – 17)

3. **His Word** (The Holy Bible – 2 Timothy 3: 16 – 17)

4. **Animals** (The Donkey – Numbers 22: 28 – 30; The Snake – Genesis 3: 1 – 4)

5. **Circumstances** (Psalm 119: 67 – 68)

6. **Environment and Signs In The Sky** (Nahum 1: 3; Job 38: 1; Psalms 19: 1 - 2)

7. **Angels** (Isaiah 6; Luke 1: 28 *Take note*: Luke 2: 19 Mary did not reject the Word)

8. **Natural Occurrences** – Fires, Floods, Earthquakes (Isaiah 66: 15)

9. **Prophecy** (1 Corinthians 1 – 11 especially Chapter 10)

10. **His Servants** (Anyone in the Fivefold according to Ephesians 4: 11)

11. **Wise Counsel** (The Book of Proverbs)

When God speaks, as He did, for example, through Jonah to Nineveh, the people called a fast, and locked the city down right away. They did not come against the Word from the Lord, nor did they reject His servant. When God speaks through the prophetic word, and the nation rejects the Word of the Lord, then the judgement of God will come upon them – Administrations lose elections, natural disasters occur, diseases, and economic collapse, just to name a few.

At one time, Jonah had refused to deliver the Word of the Lord to Nineveh as God had instructed. Many prophets refuse to carry out God's instructions the way God gave it to them to carry out. Some believe the people to whom the prophetic word must be released, are too wicked. There are others who do not want to go through the persecution so they refuse. Hence, they refuse to carry out their assignment. When we refuse to do so, God will create situations to bring you to your location. For example, in Jonah 1.

What is the Lord saying to you through your circumstances? I know that God is saying at this time, *"Backslider, return! The grace is running out."* This is especially to those with Biblical names.

Many in the Body of Christ have been counseled, but have received the wrong counsel. If you are going to see counsel, seek it from those hearing from God. Do not be

like Rehoboam – Solomon's son, who received wrong counsel, causing His administration to split and his minister die because of the people's revolt.
Many politicians, because of their refusal to listen to the voice of God, suffer and will suffer the same fate. Amos 4: 13 says, *"For behold, He who forms mountains, and creates the wind, Who declares to man what his thought is, and makes the morning darkness, Who treads the high places of the earth— The Lord God of hosts is His name."*

This shows us that the thoughts and ideas that we receive – whether we are saved or unsaved – ideas, strategies, tactics and solutions, as long as they are positive and are in line with the Word of God, it is God Who has spoken. All atheists and billionaires who are given ideas for products may think it is their intellect, but it is God Who does it.

Let it be declared that negative thoughts which promote unclean lifestyles or any other evil, would not be God but in fact the devil. God speaks to us to build us up and to give us a better life. (See Deuteronomy 8: 18). God gives us the power to get wealth, including ideas and strategies.

Dreams and Visions

1. Dreams and Visions provide answers to your questions

2. Instructs us in the things of God

3. Warns us about unseen danger

4. Guides us from wrong-doing

5. Keeps us from Pride
6. Saves our lives

The following scriptures should give some insight:

- ✓ Genesis 20: 3 – 8
- ✓ Genesis 31: 24
- ✓ Daniel 4: 19 – 37
- ✓ Matthew 1: 19 - 21
- ✓ Matthew 2: 13
- ✓ Matthew 27: 19

Security Personnel

Many times, people criticize the Voice of God, but spend a great deal to hear from other sources. There have been instances where I have personally interacted with persons in positions of influence in the security field, who are highly academically qualified in their field, and gave them the Word from the Lord that would have put them ahead of the game so-to-speak and afforded them a strategy to allow them to work better, smarter and be more effective. However, as a result of their own pride, they belittled and criticized the Source of the Word, deem the messenger a suspect and crazy and ignored the instructions. Needless to say, that was to their own demise.

We must all understand that nothing happens in the earth unless God reveals it to His servants. (Amos 3). Unless the Lord builds the house, you labor in vain who build it. (Psalm 127)

Regardless of the numerous security devices or man's qualifications, security without God is no security at all. The world cannot fight terrorism without the Spirit of God and His Voice, because He sees and knows all things. In the Bible, it was the prophet of God who instructed the kings and warned of pending attacks. (2 Kings 6). They could see and hear in the king's bedroom. As the years go by, terrorism against nations will increase, and in order to be successful in fighting and winning, they will need to depend on the servants of God. I have found that where people reject or refuse to listen to the Voice of God, they are actually afraid of the Voice of God; they are afraid of the truth being revealed. Many, especially in the churches, fight the Voice of God out of the Church – particularly the Prophetic voice, because they are covering with the wrong covering and do not want that to be revealed. As a result, they come with varying theological lies, because they want to keep the people in the deception.

Many are dying without hope when there are so many gifts existing within the Church, (Romans 12: 6 – 8), while Christians sit idle. Never attend a church which comes against the gifts or the Holy Spirit.

God is speaking, particularly about a global famine coming, and attacks.

People must:

1. Stockpile non-perishable items, toiletries and water

2. Seek the Lord before going out to places of entertainment and sporting activities

Prophecies

1 Thessalonians 5: 19 – 22 says,

"Do not quench the Spirit. Do not despise prophecies. Test all things; hold fast what is good. Abstain from every form of evil."

These words are clear. Never despise Prophecy. What we must do is test all things, hold fast to what is good. The Thessalonians were guilty of what the scriptures say above. We must test, prove and validate all charismatic activities. He never said we must quench or despise it. When we quench, we out the flame of fire which He is pouring out to bring enlightenment and healing within the Church.

People need words of direction, hope and healing. They want their purpose to manifest. When they come into the House of God, they come to be transformed by the Holy Spirit. When we hinder the move of God, we are sending people to psychics, tarot card readers, tea leaf readers and so on, to seek help, robbing the church of God.

True prophets of God lead people to change to a closer walk with God, bring enlightenment and teaching the importance of true repentance. We all need to have an expectation to hear from God on a daily basis.

I will never forget how we went through a season of wilderness in 2007. We went through lack, sickness, loss and failure. There was no one to help us. We received a prophecy through Bishop Dr. Doris Hutchinson, from the Scripture Jeremiah 29: 11 and Exodus 14: 13 respectively, which said,

"For I know the thoughts that I think toward you, says the Lord, thoughts of peace and not of evil, to give you a future and a hope."

"And Moses said to the people, "Do not be afraid. Stand still, and see the salvation of the Lord, which He will accomplish for you today. For the Egyptians whom you see today, you shall see again no more forever."

We printed it and put it on our wall. Furthermore, we received other personal prophecies during that painful season.

Imagine going through problems, a time of tests and wilderness, so much so that even you who have the gift of Prophecy cannot receive a Word from the Lord because He has gone silent on you and you do not know what to do? Why does that happen? Just remember this – a teacher never speaks when you are doing an exam; neither can you copy.

Many of you have received dreams of being in a classroom – one of the interpretations is that you are going through a test. One Prophetic will revive, encourage and restore you, and reveal to you the good things ahead, in the same way it did when Elijah was discouraged, running from Jezebel and received a Word from the Lord to gird his loins because his journey was great.

Many of you reading are on the verge of giving up, and one or two may want to commit suicide. God says "**GET UP!**" What you are going through is just a test.

God allowed me to write a book during that season called **Man, Money, Ministry**. There is nothing wrong with Prophecy; God just simply wants us to test the spirits (1 John 4: 1) to see its source.

Satan only attacks the true prophets of God. There are many people who are suffering today, and are afraid to confide in someone. They are in need of a Prophetic word through someone confidential. They need to know the will of God for their lives. Some think God has forgotten them. Prophecies bring you in alignment with heaven for your life. Many do not know their calling is in the Fivefold ministry. Not everyone is a prophet, but all have the ability to prophesy. (Acts 2: 1 – 4; Acts 19: 5 – 6).

Jesus died to give us the ability to speak in tongues and prophesy as stated in the Book of Acts. Before Jesus came into the earth, it was prophesied. (Numbers 11: 29; Isaiah 7: 14; Matthew 1: 22 – 23; Luke 2: 8 – 4 where the angel prophesied to Mary).

God is pouring out of His Spirit upon all flesh. Why reject this beautiful gift?

Predictive Prophecy

These are prophecies which come with conditions, such as in Deuteronomy 28: 1 – 14 and Leviticus 26: 3 – 4. God will give a prophetic word that He is ready to bless you, and He will also give a word of the great things that will happen in the future for you.

All these prophecies will be fulfilled when you obey the conditions, and this also go for both nations and individuals. Predictive prophecies teach, warn, and instruct you on how to walk obedience and truthful living. It is also given, to understand our confidence in God's sovereignty that He is in control and He knows the beginning and the end. When God give us a promise, and we disobey, we cancel the promises for our lives. (Leviticus 26: 14 – 16.) 2 Chronicles 7: 14 is also a predictive prophecy given to both individuals and nations.

That outlines to us the blessings and the conditions to receive from God. What we must do and what God will do. This scripture clearly outlines the dos and don'ts to receive the prophecy of God. When we failed to accept the prophecy of God, for example, when we refuse to walk in humility, we will not receive God's promise. Many will quote but failed to live up to that scripture.

Another example of predictive prophecy is found in Jonah 3 especially verses 2 – 4 about God's promise to destroy Nineveh; but because the people repented, God changed His mind. Any prophecies that are given about judgment or blessings are subject to our obedience and our repentance to the Lord. Many times, people are given prophetic words, but they refuse to carry out the conditions that are given, yet they want to blame the Prophet given the word as being false while they refuse to examine themselves because they are the ones that forfeit their prophecy. We also see in Jeremiah 18: 7 – 10, that God clearly outlined that any nation that He speaks to, concerning judgment and disaster, once we repent, He will hold back His hand.

There are also prophecies that will come to pass with no condition at all. (John 14: 3. Daniel 2: 34, Ezekiel 38, Ezekiel 39, Mathew 24, Mathew 25, and The Book of

Revelation.) All those predicted will come to pass. These are called Biblical prophecies.

Personal Prophecies

Anyone can get a personal prophecy. Personal prophecy can come in different forms. It can come through prophetic utterance by God's servant. God will pour out the Spirit of Prophecy in the end time. You can receive personal prophecies through dreams and visions. You can even receive in your church service whether to encourage you, comfort you, bring general blessings or direction. It can also be used to confirm your gift and your calling within local church. (1 Corinthians 12: 7, 1 Corinthians 14: 29 – 33, Genesis 37, Genesis 31: 11, Isaiah 6: 8.)

Chapter 21

FOLLOW GOD'S INSTRUCTIONS

Regardless of how foolish an instruction may seem, it is the key to overcoming certain obstacles in your life is, to simply follow the instructions – whether spiritual or professional. God will never give you an instruction which goes against His Word.

I have seen many persons going through problems and God gives them simple instructions in order to solve those problems. However, some start the process but then become inconsistent and ultimately cease carrying out the instruction. Meanwhile, others just ignore the instructions altogether. There are others who start the execution of the instructions but as soon as they see a little light in their circumstances, they abandon the instructions to run after the light and then because they did not follow through on the instructions, the problem returns and they are back at square one.

When problems come up, the Lord does not always use the same method to bring the solution to your situation. Not every problem requires long prayers and prophecies to get you past the problem. Some solutions come in the form of instructions from God that must be followed to get the complete breakthrough/victory. This is why the Lord has given the gifts of Word of Knowledge and Word of Wisdom – for Direction. Again, God is not going to give you instructions that are opposite to or go against His Word.

When you go to the doctor you must follow the instructions given on the prescription in order to get the full benefit of healing. In legal matters, you must follow the instructions of the lawyer in order to be victorious in your case. In the same way, when you go to the servant of God for Spiritual counseling and advice, you must also follow the instructions given. In all cases – Doctor, Lawyer, God's servant – there is time that was spent to get the necessary instruction for you to follow for your benefit; and it cost the doctor years of study and continuing education; it cost the lawyer their years of study and time to stay up-to-date with current laws in order to advise you well; and it cost the servant of God, time spent in the Presence of God, and in the Scriptures and maintaining a holy lifestyle to receive and maintain the anointing to hear from God and give you the right instructions for your situation. Your obedience to God's instructions bring peace, prosperity and the fulfillment of your purpose and also creates miracles. You will never move forward past your last act of obedience. (Deuteronomy 28: 1 – 14; Proverbs 14: 12; John 14: 21; Joshua 7: 10 – 13; 1 Kings 17: 15 – 16; Hebrews 11: 11; Ephesians 6: 5 – 8 and 2 Kings 5)

When things are not going right in your life, check and see which instructions you did not follow. What if the leprous commander Naaman did not obey the instruction to dip seven (7) times in the Jordan? What if he had allowed his pride to cause him to disobey the instructions? You will never be a good leader until you learn to follow instructions; and here is the big key – YOU DO NOT HAVE TO UNDERSTAND HIS INSTRUCTIONS. For example, a person may be acting in a movie and the director gives an instruction on how to play a part. The director sees the vision for the movie much clearer than the actor does, so the actor only needs to follow the director's instructions. Likewise, when your boss gives you an instruction on the job, your role is to follow the instructions as long as those instructions do not go against the company's policies and guidelines. You are not the boss and you are not privy to what the boss knows concerning the organization's vision.

Remember, you can be given an instruction – both spiritually and naturally – just to see if you are willing to follow instructions.

Recurring problems happen because instructions are not followed. Political and governmental failure and defeat comes about when they refuse to follow instructions. Ministerial failure comes about when people refuse to obey the instructions given by God and the leader above them. Life becomes easier when we follow God's instructions and waste is reduced and eliminated. The world would be a much better place if we only learned to follow instructions. Discipline starts with following instructions. Our victory begins when we obey and carry out the instructions given.

Chapter 22

MIRACLES AND INSTRUCTIONS

For every miracle to manifest, God always gives us an instruction to follow. In John 9: 6 – 7 it says,

"Jesus said to the man he must go and wash".

In 2 Kings 5: 1 - 19, instructions were also given by the Prophet Elisha for Namaan to bathe seven (7) times in order for him to receive miraculous healing.

Faith For The Miracle

For us to receive a miracle we must have faith in Jesus. Whenever we call on the name of Jesus, Acts 3: 16 reminds us that we must believe. Faith is what moves God to release a miracle on our behalf. For example, a simple action such as writing our debts on paper and burning it to prophetically represent debt cancellation, can create a miracle.

Additionally, Mark 11 and Proverbs 18: 21 also remind us that the words we speak can create a miracle. If you are sick, begin to speak and declare healing in your body; declare that cycles, poverty, and witchcraft be broken. There are miracles in our mouths.

Furthermore, a small seed can create a miracle. We see that happening in Matthew 14: 13 – 21 where the five (5) loaves and two (2) fishes given as a seed by the little boy, created a miracle that could feed 5000. Jesus teaches us that we must always look up to God for a miracle. As we look to God our Source, He will give us miracles for creative finance – the necessary wealth, resources, tactics and strategies to distribute resources to the multitudes. God may give you a vision to feed the poor, but in order to deal with the need of the people we must look to God for miracle.

Look To God

When we look to God, He will show us what the most important thing in our midst to bring change. For example, the homeless, the fatherless, the poor, they may be considered the fragments or crumbs of the society – the *"leftovers"*; but when we pick them up, we bring change within the society.

Many times, we miss out on miracle, because we failed to follow instructions. Each day without fail, God presents benefits, but we often miss these benefits of God, because we refuse to obey God's instructions. Nations and individuals suffer because they failed to follow instruction.

The question is, what if God says to you, "go and dip seven (7) times in some unknown river to get your healing?" For most people it would not seem logical, and they would begin to question how clean the river is or if there isn't one closer to them; but they would have a difficult time receiving a miracle from God. Miracles comes through faith in God and we are all entitled to receive miracles – so then receiving our miracle(s) become a matter of choice – our choice.

Sometimes, miracles do not come in the way we are looking. God may instruct us to do something that does not make sense to the natural mind, but if we trust Him and the instructions He gives, we will see the miracle manifest. We cannot continue to analyze spiritual matters with the natural or logical way of thinking; logic and faith do not work together. Jesus spat on the clay and anointed a blind man eye. He received miracle. A person who dipped seven (7) times in the sea received a miracle.

What instructions have you received from God, but did not follow, because it did not make sense to you? Could that have been a moment for a miracle you needed? Are you willing to write the amount you are asking the Lord for on a bank withdrawal slip by faith? Or fill out a western union slip to receive money, or write on an envelope and believe by faith?

Point Of Contact

From time to time, a prophetic act may require using an item – usually personal – as a point of contact, a symbolic connection to the owner (or prospective owner) in their physical absence, in order to request a miracle or to create the environment for their miracle from God on their behalf where they are not in the position to do so themselves.

In Acts 19, Paul the Apostle use a handkerchief as a point of contact to create miracle. So, we can use something, for example, a handkerchief, shirt, key, dress, as a point of contact to create miracle.

What if you receive a letter with bad news? In 2 Kings 19: 14 – 15, the king received a letter with bad news. He spread it before the Lord as a point of contact and received a miracle. In times of adversity, we must always "spread out" our trouble before God. (Read also Isaiah 37: 14 – 21).

Other Ways to Receive Miracles

Do not be afraid to pray and seek God first for miracles when problems arise. God uses simple things to bring miracle to you.

1. Prayer and Fasting bring miracles.

2. Paying Tithes and Sowing Seed/Giving bring miracles.

3. Following God's instructions brings miracles.

As long as you are in Fivefold Ministry, you must always believe in miracles, seek God for miracles, expect miracles, and understand that miracles are real.

Grace for Miracles

Everything we want to do through Jesus Christ, we only can successfully achieve it through His divine Grace. If you want favor, you are going to need grace, if you want miracles, you will need grace, if you want great power you are going to need Grace. Great grace allows us to witness to the resurrection of the Lord. (Acts 4: 33.)

Through Grace comes the following:
        1) Energy
        2) Power
        3) Might
        4) Great Force, Ability and Strength.

Great grace brings the *Dunamis* power which brings transformation, increase, God's presence, mountains and obstacles to remove in our church and our daily activity. When great grace begins to fall, lack and poverty begin to go, people will begin to give willingly, as in the books of Acts, we see people begin to sell their resources and begin to give to the church. And God begins to add to new members to the church daily. He also begins to empower the Apostles to flow in miracles, signs and wonders. We also begin to see unity manifest in the church. None of these could take place without grace. We are even seeing great grace fall when Peter's very shadow begins to bring great healing and miracle. (Acts 5: 14 – 16.) In Acts 6, we also see where the manifestation of God's Grace and Miracles were on Deacon Stephen.

Grace allowed water to be turned into wine. There is a need for increase of grace and miracle within Fivefold Ministry to deal with the resources that are needed to reap the harvest in the end time. (John 2: 1 – 11.)

We have come to the point in our global society where we are trying to make things happen on our own – we try to create our own blessings. We are no longer looking to God to grant us the miracle or breakthrough. Where there is no demand, there is no need for a supply. When there is a demand for miracles, signs and wonders within the local church, then miracles will begin to happen again. We must, therefore, stir up our faith in God, and with that create an environment for miracles to happen within the local church. Some people believe only when they see signs and wonders, but we must believe in Jesus, before we see signs and wonders. And we will see salvation begin to manifest within our church, our community, our nation.

We are people of faith. Faith is the action, while Grace is the manifestation. You turn on a pipe by faith, but the water that comes out is grace. A person who sits down in church doing nothing, they will not access the grace that is given. Everything we do, we do by faith, we tithe by faith, we receive by grace, we accept Jesus by faith, and we are saved by grace. Grace is the gift of God; Grace is unmerited favor. No one can be saved without God's grace, but that person must believe and accept Him by faith. Then they will receive the benefits. Everything we need in life; it has to do with God's grace. There are many millionaires within the society. It is true that it is not their hard work that brings them to that millionaire status. It is God's grace. Each time we pray to God for His blessings and to change our circumstances, to change the condition of our church, what He does is increasing His grace upon us. What we need in an increase in God's grace.

Chapter 23

MORE ON THE GIFTS

Word of Knowledge and Prophecy

Spiritual gifts are very important, so it is critical for us to learn as much as possible about them. You will not learn overnight, you will learn more as you grow more in God. Oftentimes people ask, *"What is the difference between the gifts of Prophecy and Word of Knowledge?"*

Prophecies deal with the future – what is to come; while the gift of Word of Knowledge speaks of the past and present. Sometimes, people confuse the two (2). For example, John 1: 48 was Jesus Christ giving a Word of Knowledge. Also, in John 2: 16 – 20, when Jesus spoke to the woman at the well, He was able to tell her the current situation in and state of her life. In 2 Kings 5, Elisha saw in the spirit that Gehazi was taking money from Naaman at that same moment he saw it. The Prophet Samuel could identify where Saul's donkey was, when Saul's men were searching for it.

Word of Knowledge is the supernatural revelation of something you would not ordinarily know at the natural level. We need more people with the gift of Word of Knowledge. Please note that a person may have the gift of Word of Knowledge, but he/she is not a prophet.

A prophet is a 24-hour office according to Ephesians 4: 11. To walk in accuracy, it is critical for us to pray that the Word of Knowledge will manifest. It is critical in this end-time for all the major prophets function in that gift.

In John 8: 13 – 20, Jesus began to reveal the secrets of the accusers who wanted to stone the woman they accused of adultery.

A person with Word of Knowledge should never utilize this gift to manipulate, expose or extort anyone; nor should we use this gift to destroy any church/church leader. This gift is to be used for edification, healing and clarity. It is good also for counseling sessions. Intercessors need it to deal with sensitive issues.

In Acts 8, Peter used this gift to reveal the heart of Simon the Sorcerer. There are many people within the local church, who are covered with an un-Godly covering.

Word of Knowledge can be used in espionage, intelligence gathering, according to 2 Kings 6, and can defeat the enemy.

Remember, the Past and Present deal with the Word of Knowledge. But if someone tells you, "The Lord is about to release a blessing to you, it is a Prophecy; and it is for comfort, edification, and exhortation. Question: What if someone comes to kill or poison you, which gift would you need, Word of Knowledge or Discernment of Spirits? You will need Word of Knowledge to reveal the past or present and then the Discernment of Spirits will reveal the motives, spirit and intention.

Word of Wisdom

The Gift of Word of Wisdom tells the future actions necessary to accompany or deal with the prophetic word uttered – to solve mysteries, and give solutions as well as protect from loss. For example, if we are given the prophetic word that there will be a famine, then we have received the Prophecy. However, we will need to know what to do and how to prepare for the famine in order to prevent loss of life and extreme and widespread starvation and all that comes with it. The Lord, Who sees and knows all things, therefore releases the Word of Wisdom so that we can formulate plans for what lies ahead and solve the problem.

Wisdom is the ability to judge which aspect of knowledge is true and how it should be applied. It is safe to say that the Gift of Word of Wisdom, is a level of foresight which tells us what to do, when to do it and how to do it.

In Genesis 41, after interpreting the Pharaoh's dreams, Joseph, through the Gift of Word of Wisdom, was able to give the Pharaoh strategies to deal with the famine that would have affected not just the nation, but the region.

In 2010, many prophets prophesied that there would be a recession, but the Body of Christ missed the opportunities to capitalize on it and many of them experienced heavy losses – losing houses, church buildings, vehicles and running into serious debt. While many were caught up with prophecies, no one listened for the Word of Wisdom to be released so they could make the necessary preparations to avoid the losses.

Now we are in a new decade, and the world is about to go through another recession and a famine. We need the Word of Wisdom to know how to prepare and what we need to prepare – whether it may be water, food, Bibles, first aid items, medication and toiletries. We need to know - will gold be the new currency, or will water become the new gold?

It is critical also, when getting into business relationships and in some cases a marital relationship, to protect your assets. In the case of business, such protections need to be included in a contract. In the case of a marriage, where there is doubt between the husband and wife to be, a simple pre-nuptial agreement can be put in place in the event of a break in the relationship.

Every one of the gifts is important. Never think you are superior to others when you have been blessed to have a gift. 1 Corinthians 12: 6 – 8 says

"And there are diversities of activities, but it is the same God who works all in all. But the manifestation of the Spirit is given to each one for the profit of all: for to one is given the word of wisdom through the Spirit, to another the word of knowledge through the same Spirit,"

Every part of the body - organs, muscles, nerves, blood – every part has its role to play. Some may take the anus for granted, however, it is shut up or if a person was born without one, how would waste be removed from their bodies? Their bodies would become toxic and die.

There are many teachings in the Body of Christ which are not Biblically correct: Prophets are teaching that they are the head of the Church and that they are superior to Apostles. They need to understand that there was no church in the Old Testament. The Church was birthed and reformed in the New Testament; bringing in the Fivefold Ministry as is seen in Ephesians 4: 11 and 1 Corinthians 12: 28 which says,

"And God has appointed these in the church: first apostles, second prophets, third teachers, after that miracles, then gifts of healings, helps, administrations, varieties of tongues."

Whenever there is a Prophet in your church who refuses to submit, ask them, *"To whom are you accountable?"*

Signs and Wonders

We need Signs and Wonders in the Church. However, these can be a hindrance to our faith. Many will not want to obey unless they see signs and wonders. John 4: 48 says, *"Then Jesus said to him, "Unless you people see signs and wonders, you will by no means believe."* Many refuse to accept the Lord as Savior because they want to see something first before they believe Him or in Him. By reading the Bible we see that you must utilize faith in order to receive the grace. (Romans 10: 9 – 10).

Salvation is a miracle, and it is also a sign and a wonder. In 1 Kings 17, we see miracles, signs and wonders take place because the widow obeyed even before she saw the signs and wonders and she received. There are many who are sick and are unable to receive healing, because they want to see a sign or wonder before they believe.

In Acts 19: 11 – 12 we see unusual miracles take place involving Paul the Apostle, where handkerchiefs or aprons were brought from his body to the sick and they were healed.

When the mere shadow of Apostle Peter passed, people on the streets began receiving healing.

Acts 28: 2 – 9, reveal more signs and wonders with Paul, which brought great provision so there would be no lack.

Signs and Wonders must glorify God, not man. Many are touching God's glory and if we as members of the Fivefold are not rooted and grounded in God, many will fall away by false Signs and Wonders. 2 Thessalonians 2: 9 says,

<u>"The coming of the lawless one is according to the working of Satan, with all power, signs, and lying wonders,"</u>

Matthew 24: 24 also says,

"For false christs and false prophets will rise and show great signs and wonders to deceive, if possible, even the elect."

Finally, Revelation 16: 14 tells us,
"For they are spirits of demons, performing signs, which go out to the kings of the earth and of the whole world, to gather them to the battle of that great day of God Almighty."

Many people become extremely ecstatic at the sight of a little gold dust or a little oil appear on the person speaking to them and declare that because of that, they are seeing a true man of God in action – without testing the spirits at work. Meanwhile, God wants to manifest through His

Apostles and other Fivefold personnel. It is critical, according to Romans 15: 19 – 21, for us to discern.

God will be pouring out a mighty grace in the end-time to reap the harvest upon those who are genuine. Many of God's servants will need to confront the enemy, as Paul did. There will be a fight on for souls in the end-time. God is not in the business of coming second. God will fill heaven and the agents of Satan will feel it at the same time; and those who are in the Church, pretending to be agents of the Lord, when they are in fact servants of Satan, will be confronted by the Truth and be exposed by the Lord.

There are many communities that are bewitched and under the spells of witchcraft and God is going to anoint and use those who are willing to declare His truths and speak as He gives them the utterance just as He did with Stephen in Acts 6: 8 – 10.

Chapter 24

PREDESTINED FOR PURPOSE

Knowing your calling allows you to walk in the right path and that includes career path – starting a business, choosing to engage in the arts rather than science and so on. Please note that knowing your calling in the Fivefold is not confined to functioning in a Ministry or at a Spiritual level but includes functioning in secular society. God does not give gifts based on which area of society you function, you were predestined with gifts.

There are many today who feel that their career/chosen path is their purpose, but that is not so. For the most part, there are many whose career path has nothing to do with their purpose - the things that God has created you to do. Their purpose is not being fulfilled and that is why they are unhappy, lack joy and are struggling today. Many die without fulfilling what God created them to do, because oftentimes they were more interested in pursuing material gain. Our cemeteries are filled with the remains of people with unfulfilled purpose.

All Have Gifts and Talents

God created us all with gifts, talents and solutions to change the world. It is critical for us to bring it forth. But in doing so, many are afraid to start small, when we are told not to forsake or despise small beginnings. Fulfilling God's purpose is the only way we will experience real joy.

Oftentimes people confuse happiness and joy, but they are two different experiences. Happiness is momentary and external. We can be happy and still not experience joy. Joy is lasting and reaches a deeper place within us. It is an internal fruit and only the Holy Spirit can allow you to experience joy, because it comes as a result of being in God's will.

Many may have billions and be happy about it, but still have no joy, because they are not fulfilling God's purpose for their lives.

Predestined

Why do you believe people are so angry when it comes on to injustice? It may be because God has predestined them to be a lawyer, a judge, or a civil rights leader. What about those who hate to see people sick? Maybe they were predestined to be a doctor, nurse or other health professional, or maybe they have the gift of healing and do not know it yet. There are those who hate to see people poor or lacking basic necessities of life. They may be predestined to own and operate large humanitarian centers to help the poor. There are many within the political arena who should be functioning within ministry, and there are many in ministry who should be functioning in politics or some other area of government.

The word *"predestined"* is a word we may have either heard or read in the Scriptures before but, many may not full grasp what it means for us in the grand scheme of things. Romans 9: 28 – 30 says,

"And we know that all things work together for good to those who love God, to those who are the called according to His purpose. For whom He foreknew, He also predestined to be conformed to the image of His Son, that He might be the firstborn among many brethren. Moreover, whom He predestined, these He also called; whom He called, these He also justified; and whom He justified, these He also glorified." (See also Ephesians 1: 5)

There are times things happen to us for which we never bargained. We may also be disappointed or lacking in joy each day we are in a profession that does not bring us satisfaction, and then we realize that there has to be more than where we are. There may be people who are unsaved, or are atheists, or lawmakers determined to put things in place to stop the growth of Christianity. But deep within, they realize that something is not adding up. You were with Christ from before the foundation of the earth, which means that He wants us to be in His image, walk righteous, holy – believing in the things He believes.

"...For whom He foreknew, He also predestined to be conformed to the image of His Son, that He might be the firstborn among many brethren..."

This tells us that before we were born into this world, we were with Him, made to be conformed to HIS image. We must align to our true identity – who we were before we were born here. That is why the fight is so great. Only through salvation – a spiritual birth – will our eyes be opened so that we can begin walking into what we were predestined to be.

This establishes the fact that God predestined us based on His foreknowledge of us. The word predestined comes from the merging of two Greek words – *"prohorizo"*. *"Pro"* means "in front" in a spatial sense or "before" in a temporal sense. *"Horizo"* means "to determine or ordain" or "to appoint."

You may be in a common-law relationship, being poorly treated; but you are royalty. You may be a janitor, but you were predestined to be wealthier than Bill Gates; or you might have made the mistake of marrying the wrong person. You may be predestined to be a prophet, but you are in the wrong profession. Life and Purpose were decided before physical birth - that is why God hates abortion.

Spiritual Gifts For The Marketplace

The Spirit of Prophecy and Word of Knowledge are tools God uses to reveal one's pre-destined purpose. There are persons who saw themselves as just another average Joe, when the Lord revealed their purpose/calling, they did not embrace it initially. But the moment they did, everything fell into place. I met a lawyer once, but the Lord told him *"you are the Mayor."* He did not fully embrace it at first, but when he did and ran for office in less than a year, he became the Mayor.

We are predestined for greatness with all the *pneumatikos* blessings (Ephesians 1: 1 – 6), that is everything we needed from the foundation of the earth.

1 Corinthians 2: 9 reminds us,

"Eye has not seen, nor ear heard, nor have entered into the heart of man the things which God has prepared for those who love Him."

There are many within the society that are fighting for power, but the question is, are you predestined for that position you are pursuing?

Born With Purpose

There is a cure, vision, revelation or solution within your DNA to come forth to help mankind, and you need to unlock it. Every person that has been born in this world was born for a purpose, born with specific instructions embedded within us. Each is unique, special and your life is valuable. You were born to make a difference.

For example, now is the opportune time to start that business. It is not your mind telling you to start that business, it is God pushing and encouraging you to bring out what He placed within you. Do not allow fear, fear of failure, obstacles or the criticisms of others to hinder you from bringing out what God has put in you.

Things to Remember

By principle, everything in life - much like a tree - starts with a seed. It means, regardless of how small, you must start from somewhere. You plant it, cover it with the soil, you water it, watch it, fight even the elements for it and it begins to shoot up as a tender plant. You begin to believe in it.

Recognize that in life, betrayal, disappointment and discouragement will come. At times, you may even feel so discouraged - as if you are not making a difference - and you may even think you should give up on that vision because it seems dead. Some people will even tell you that you missed it and you should try something else. But what you did not know is that the seed you planted by stepping out and starting the journey and going through the disappointments, discouragements and betrayals were taking deep root in the ground.

God uses your struggles to allow you to become stronger and wiser. He uses your challenges to develop you into a great tree. A great tree is about to come forth from the small seed. The seed/plant goes through infancy, youth, prime, senior, twilight - much like you and I. One day you are going to get up and see the change in effect - that the small seed brought major expansion.

Stages

There may be people at different stages - some at the infancy stage, youth or twilight - not in age, but in the process of fulfilling your purpose. It is time to monitor the tree's base, check for foundational problems, trim the tree and allow the tree to bear.

From great tests come great vision. Always remember that a tree goes through different stages, so do not give up on your vision. Keep ploughing and fighting, you have to first believe in your vision before others can believe in your product.

A time is coming that the loan they refused to give you and the help that you asked for and did not get, are the best things to happen to you, because when you reap the success, then no one but God can get the glory for it.

A person is never too old to start fulfilling his/her purpose. What are the things that burden or hurt you? These are clues to help you identify your purpose and to stir you into action. When you are fulfilling your purpose, it is more than just accomplishing a task - you are actually saving lives.

Know your calling and fulfil your purpose.

ACTIVITY 1: TEST YOUR KNOWLEDGE

True or False

1. By their fruit you shall know them T [ ] F [ ]

2. A false prophet is one who pulls people to him/herself T [ ] F [ ]

3. A false prophet denies Jesus came in the flesh T [ ] F [ ]

4. A true prophet must glorify God at all times T [ ] F [ ]

5. Prophecy must edify the Church T [ ] F [ ]

6. Prophecy must bring edification and comfort T [ ] F [ ]

7. Prophecy speaks to us about the past and the present T [ ] F [ ]

8. Word of Knowledge speaks to us about the past and the present T [ ] F [ ]

9. Any prophecy given must agree with the Word of God T [ ] F [ ]

10. Every prophet must be judged by accuracy T [ ] F [ ]

11. It is Accuracy, not the Fruit of the Spirit, that is used to determine a true prophet from the false prophet. T [ ] F [ ]

12. There are seven (7) gifts of the Holy Spirit T [ ] F [ ]

ACTIVITY 2: WRITE THE PROPHETIC WORD

Make a start. Write and date what the Lord says to you.

ACTIVITY 3: RECORD THE DREAMS YOU GET

Remember to record and date the dreams you receive from God.

_____

_____

_____

_____

_____

_____

_____

_____

_____

_____

_____

BIBLIOGRAPHY

Hagee, John C. General Editor, *Prophecy Study Bible*, (New King James Version) © 1997 Thomas Nelson, Inc

Hayford, Jack W. Executive Editor, *New Spirit-Filled Life® Bible*, (New King James Version) © 2002 Thomas Nelson, Inc.

Lyston, Michelle, *In His Presence Maintaining The Presence Of God Through Worship*, (Revised Edition) © 2012 2018 Lyston Consultancy & Enterprises LLC

Lyston, Steve, *Man, Money, Ministry*, © 2009 Xlibris

Pfeiffer, Charles F., Vos, Howard F., Rea, John. Editors, *Wycliffe Bible Dictionary*, (Seventh Printing) © 2005 Hendrickson Publishers, Inc

Price, Paula A. (PhD). *The Prophet's Dictionary: The Ultimate Guide To Supernatural Wisdom*, © 1999, 2002, 2006 Whittaker House

Strong, James. *The New Strong's Expanded Exhaustive Concordance of the Bible*, (Red Letter Edition) © 1990 Thomas Nelson Publishers

Concise Oxford English Dictionary Eleventh Edition. © 1964, 1976, 1982, 1990, 1995, 1999, 2001, 2004 Oxford University Press. All Rights Reserved.

https://www.britannica.com/topic/KGB

https://www.britannica.com/topic/Mossad

https://www.britannica.com/topic/Scotland-Yard

https://www.dictionary.com/browse/father?s=t

https://www.interpol.int/en/Who-we-are/What-is-INTERPOL

www.ingramcontent.com/pod-product-compliance
Lightning Source LLC
Chambersburg PA
CBHW061641040426
42446CB00010B/1518